# THE ENGLISH
# VILLAGE

# THE ENGLISH VILLAGE

### LEIGH DRIVER
*Photography by*
### CHRIS COE

NEW HOLLAND

First published in 2005 by New Holland Publishers (UK) Ltd
London • Cape Town • Sydney • Auckland

www.newhollandpublishers.com

Garfield House, 86–88 Edgware Road, London, W2 2EA, UK

80 McKenzie Street, Cape Town 8001, South Africa

Level 1/Unit 4, 14 Aquatic Drive, Frenchs Forest, NSW 2086, Australia

218 Lake Road, Northcote, Auckland, New Zealand

Copyright © 2005 in text: Leigh Driver
Copyright © 2005 in photographs: Chris Coe
Copyright © New Holland Publishers (UK) Ltd

10 9 8 7 6 5 4 3 2 1

ISBN 1 84330 968 8

Publishing Manager: Jo Hemmings
Senior Editor: Charlotte Judet
Designer: Rebecca Willis
Production: Joan Woodroffe


Reproduction by Pica Digital Pte Ltd, Singapore
Printed and bound by Kyodo Printing Co Pte Ltd, Singapore

## Cover and Prelim Pages

Front Cover: Thornton Le Dale, North Yorkshire
Spine: Whitburn, Tyne & Wear
Back Cover: Great Tew, Oxfordshire (left); Monks Eleigh, Suffolk (centre); Robin Hood's Bay, North Yorkshire (right).
Page 2: Longstock, Hampshire
Page 5: Selworthy, Somerset
Page 6: Chiddingfold, Surrey (top); Castle Combe, Wiltshire (middle); Monks Eleigh, Suffolk (bottom)
Page 7: Honington, Warwickshire (top): Weobley, Herefordshire (middle); Blanchland, Northumberland (bottom)
Page 9: Fingest, Buckinghamshire
Page 10: East Garston, Berkshire
Page 13: Polperro, Cornwall

## Acknowledgements

I have met with many acts of kindness whilst researching and writing this book. Villagers from every part of the country have taken the time to share with me their local knowledge and unique insight into the life and history of the villages that I visited. I would especially like to thank the staff of the Surrey History Service; Amberley Castle; Honington Hall; Westmill Tea Room; the Tudor Lodge Gift Shop, Chilham; Corn Craft, Monks Eleigh; the Village Store, East Garston; Polperro Heritage Museum; Ye Olde Bell Stores, Okeford Fitzpaine; the Wycoller Craft Centre; the Falkland Arms, Great Tew; the Snowshill Arms, Snowshill; the George and the Red Lion, Stevington; the George and Dragon, Great Budworth; the Lord Crewe Arms, Blanchland; the Star and the George, Alfriston; Mrs Joan Wade, custodian of Blakeney Guildhall; William Torrens, Buckinghamshire Local Studies; Diana Boston, the Manor, Hemingford Grey; Mr John Garner, Godwick; Mr G. Hodgkinson, Monks Eleigh; Mr G Hawthorn, Woodbastwick; Susan Walmsley, Clitheroe Tourist Information Centre; Colin and Patricia Haggar, Exton; Tom Doig and Stephen Ruff, Westmill; Mr & Mrs Smith, Symonds, Dunsford and local historians Marion Ellis, (Braceby); Mavis Backhouse, (Westmill); Sybil Reeder (Whitburn); Anne Maltby (Kersey) and Thelma Blake (Great Milton).

Thanks must also go to Charlotte, my editor, for her expert guidance and seemingly inexhaustible patience and to Chris for the wonderful photographs.

But I owe the greatest debt of all to my family. To Jason and my children, Stephen, Daniel and Michael, for their tireless support and encouragement; to my sister Beverley for her invaluable advice; to my late mother, whose infectious enthusiasm for 'day trips to interesting places' inspired in me a life-long love of history and the English village, and above all to my father who made all things possible.

# CONTENTS

Foreword 8

Introduction 10

## The South and South East 14

## The South West 46

# The Eastern Counties 80

# Central England & the West 118

# The Northern Counties 156

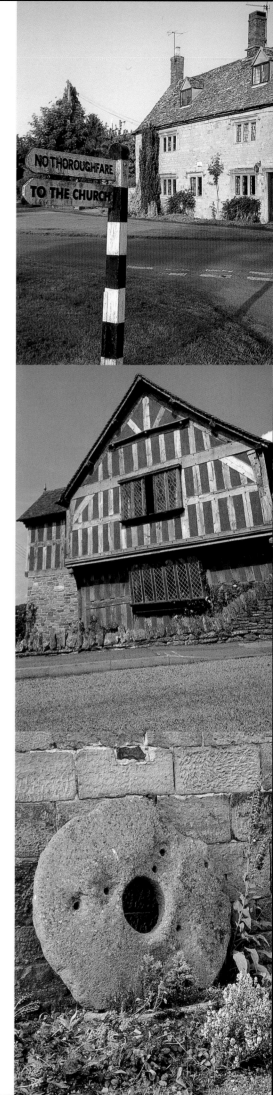

# FOREWORD

In our hearts many of us feel that we are children of the English village, and not without some justification. Before the Industrial Revolution engendered the rise of great towns and cities all over the country, nearly three-quarters of England's population lived in villages, hamlets and scattered farmsteads.

Those who have been able to trace their ancestry back to the England of the 18th century or even earlier more often than not discover that their forebears resided in an English village. Yet even people without such a connection, unquestionably in the majority, are still quite likely to meet any mention of the 'English village' with responses ranging from enthusiastic appreciation to total bewilderment as to why the smallest rural settlements of England should be held in such high regard; yet almost never do they express indifference.

This book sets out to investigate the origins and importance of English villages: why they developed where they did; why they look as they do; and why it is that, both collectively and individually, they elicit such a strong emotional response, even in people who have never seen one at first hand. The book will also tell the stories of some of the villagers who brought these diverse settlements to life, and explore their local lore and traditions, their pastimes and crafts. Finally, it will endeavour to reconnect the intangible myth with the physical reality in a search for the 'quintessential English village'.

One could be forgiven for regarding the last of these objectives with a degree of scepticism, for not only is the definition of what actually constitutes a 'village' uncertain at best, no two villages are the same. There are well recognized regional differences in the building materials available to the craftsmen who have fashioned and refashioned the fabric of our settlements over the centuries. In addition, there are also local peculiarities of origin, form, site and function. This seemingly infinite variety, while essential to the charm of the English village, clearly makes the task of uncovering the identity of one that could be described as 'quintessential' that much more of a challenge.

Furthermore, it seems that we each cherish our own personal vision of what such a village should be like. Nevertheless, whether this mental image has been formed through personal experience, by reading literary works of fact or fiction, or through the media of television, film, radio, wall calendars or even bedtime stories read to us in childhood, it will generally contain two or more of the following elements: a green, pond, church, inn and cottages, with possibly a shop, school or manor house thrown in for good measure.

In pursuit of some insight into the phenomenon of the English village, and in an attempt to unravel the mystery of the spell it has cast over us I have travelled the length and breadth of the country, exploring its broad highways and narrow lanes in search of the roots of this deepest of connections. The result is that, with some considerable difficulty, I have reduced more than 13,000 villages to a broadly representative (but undeniably subjective) shortlist of 86 of the best examples I think this country has to offer.

Constraints on space and the desire to include a fairly even spread of examples across the country have meant that sometimes villages situated in counties rich in examples of beauty and charm have not made it into the final selection, whereas some slightly less attractive settlements from areas not so blessed have been included. Issues of fairness and personal preference aside, I think you'll agree that every example of an English village to be found within the pages of this book has outstanding merits which make it worthy of inclusion.

But did I discover the *quintessential* English village? Read on and you will find out.

# INTRODUCTION

Various physical elements of village life such as the green, pond, pump, well, church, inn, manor house, mill and cottage will be examined in context over the pages that follow, but there are some general points that perhaps should be considered first.

## What is a village?

It would seem that there is no real definition of a village, or at least none that is broadly acceptable to most villagers. There are those who insist that a village must have more than a handful of cottages, that there should at least be a church or that there is a required degree

of self-sufficiency but not too much prosperity, for should the settlement grow large or gain a market it would then become a town.

Accidents of geography that suddenly placed the resources of humble settlements in step with the requirements of their age resulted in some villages becoming towns. Then, when the focus of the economy changed (as it so often does), many reverted to being villages once more – some more graciously than others. Today, there are communities ranging from a few dozen inhabitants to more than 6,000, all of whom claim to live in a village. So perhaps then the definition of a village is actually very simple for it would seem that, despite the best efforts of lexicographers and even the British Government, a village is a village if the people living there say that it is.

## Origins

Although the Saxons are usually credited with bringing the village to England, 1,500 years or so before their systematic colonization of this country began Iron Age Celts had already developed an integrated system of settlement and farming. However, their small, isolated farmsteads generally have left but faint traces on the landscape, whereas the Saxons laid down a pattern of occupation that largely persists today. They also put in place systems of government, justice and taxation so effective that when the Normans invaded in the 11th century, they simply adapted a system that had been working well for centuries.

Under the Norman feudal system of manorial organization, which centred on the concept of mutual obligation, those in the upper reaches of the clearly defined social order provided land and protection to those below in return for labour and services. Initially imposed from a position of military strength, the system gradually became familiar enough for its profound inequalities to be thought of as the 'natural order' of things. This is not to suggest that everyone was content with their lot, but the belief that the benefits of social stability far outweighed the hardships of extreme poverty and virtual slavery suffered by a large proportion of the population seems to have prevailed.

## Siting

By the time of the Norman Conquest, the vast majority of the villages that we know today were already in existence. Whereas the Celts had a clear preference for high valley slopes and hilltops, the Saxons were more inclined to seek out prime spots in lower-lying areas. However, when choosing a site for permanent settlement, many factors would have been taken into account. Considerations such as a sheltered position, the availability of fertile land, a ready supply of building materials, and (in coastal areas) access to a safe harbour for fishing or waterborne trade, may each have played their part. Perhaps the presence of a ford across a river, the discovery of easily workable mineral deposits or the proximity of a defensive fortification might encourage a group of people to put down roots, but the one thing that no community could possibly do without was a reliable source of fresh water.

## Form

Several different types of village have been identified. Those that have grown up around an obvious focal point such as a green or a church have been designated 'nuclear' villages. They are usually compact, with lanes and tracks radiating out from a focal point to connect with the fields all around. There are also settlements with multiple nuclei, which are known as 'polyfocal' villages, while those without any discernible focus are termed 'scattered', often being formed when individual farmsteads were joined over time by the gradual removal of the vegetation that separated them. A 'linear' village is one that has spread itself along riverbank or roadside, a further development of this being the settlement at a crossroads or major junction. To these must be added planned, or 'model', villages, all the

houses being built within a relatively short period of time, usually to accommodate estate or industrial workers.

Yet the English village stubbornly defies any attempt at definitive classification. With the majority of humbler dwellings being constructed roughly and of perishable materials, they would usually need to be rebuilt every 30–40 years. Even stone villages were known to shift and change shape – the salvageable material from derelict structures being incorporated into the new. Thus, the focus and outline of a village would be constantly changing; contracting or expanding as its economy fluctuated or outbreaks of disease came and went.

## Fluctuating fortunes

Until quite recently, most villages were basically self-sufficient. Yet pressures and influences within the country as a whole have meant that throughout its history a village may have experienced several notable changes of fortune. In the aftermath of the Black Death, when the population of 14th-century England had been reduced by up to 50 percent, there was plenty of available land but precious few men to work it, thereby effectively putting an end to the centuries-old feudal system. There was now sufficient land for some of it to be held in common by the villagers in order that they could graze their livestock freely and gather fuel. For a brief period, it seemed that the humble agricultural labourer had finally gained the upper hand, commanding higher prices for his services and demanding to be treated with more consideration. But it was not to last. To increase productivity and reduce costs, many landowners turned their arable land over to sheep farming, which required much less manpower and yet yielded a far greater return. Sometimes whole villages were cleared away to make way for extensive sheep walks, and the welfare of the villagers, most of whom were now surplus to requirements, seems often to have been of little importance. Before long, the vast open fields with their many small strips of land so typical of lowland areas were unable to keep pace with the ever-increasing demand for food from the growing towns. In the name of efficiency, landowners sought enclosure awards of the government, by which they divided the open fields and much of the common land between them, thus creating large private estates. Villagers, now denied access to their grazing land and fuel, were offered small 'allotments' by way of compensation, yet often this particular detail seems to have been forgotten when the plans became reality. For the first time in many lowland areas, boundaries such as hedges, fences and walls were put up around small fields, altering the face of the local landscape. Farmers moved out of the village to be closer to their land. Many villagers left, too, since moving to town now seemed the only alternative to starvation. Those that remained found that they were powerless once more. Periods of agricultural depression saw wages cut to the point where, if they had fallen any lower, the labourer would not have had the strength to work. Gradually, the 'push' of the desperate situation in the countryside, combined with the 'pull' of perceived opportunities in the town, left the typical English village nearly empty. Only then, with the all-important food supply to the towns under threat, did the government act to staunch the flow of people. However, by then it was already too late for many rural communities.

Villages were allowed to decay for many years. It was only in the 1950s, when motoring holidays became possible for the masses and city dwellers began to look for weekend retreats in the country, that large numbers of semi-derelict rural properties were snapped up at bargain prices and lovingly restored; yet countless more had been lost.

## Community

For most villages, the cooperative efforts of family, friends and neighbours have been essential to the settlement's survival. In medieval times, expensive implements and beasts beyond the pocket of any one villager would be pooled; for instance, there might be a 'village plough', perhaps kept at the church, and in late summer the whole village would turn out to ensure the harvest was brought safely in. In a small, closely knit society where there was no social provision for sickness or injury, a support network of friends and neighbours could make all the difference. With no organized police force, it fell to the villagers to look out for each other's property and to apprehend any malefactor.

It would be wrong, however, to suggest universal harmony. There were disputes between villagers, just as there are today, and there were people whose behaviour occasionally offended the accepted moral code of a community compelled to attend church on a Sunday, whether they understood the proceedings there or not. So-called 'rough music' – a form of cat-calling accompanied by the clattering of pots and pans – could be used by a mob to punish someone or even hound them out of the village altogether.

There was a clearly defined social hierarchy operating in all villages, headed in most cases by the lord of the manor (or the 'squire'). In the absence of such a figure, the rector or vicar would take on the role of principal inhabitant. If it was a small village with no resident doctor or solicitor, the farmers would be next in importance, followed by the schoolmaster if there was one, the miller, the innkeeper and local craftsmen such as the blacksmith, carpenter, wheelwright, saddler, builder, thatcher and stone-mason. The social position of shopkeepers was variable: sometimes they were 'above' the craftsmen, for shop work was not strictly working with your hands, and sometimes they were 'below', since it was considered that the job required no special knowledge or skill, although butchers and bakers fell somewhere between the two. After the carter, or carrier, who transported both people and goods, would come the labourers, with those who had specialized roles, such as horse men, dairy men and shepherds, taking precedence over the generally unskilled but often multitalented labourers.

Everyone in the village knew their 'place' the order of the womenfolk mostly following that of the men to whom they were related but a special place would be reserved for the midwife. Usually with no medical training, her only qualification might have been that she had successfully given birth to a number of children herself. Perhaps she would be the one who was called out to nurse the sick and lay out the dead, and maybe she was also the village authority on folk remedies. In the days before antibiotics, these natural cures were gathered from the surrounding fields and hedgerows or grown in the cottage garden; some have now been found to have real medicinal properties. Often these natural cures could be more effective – particularly when accompanied by a sizeable dose of superstition – than anything the local doctor could do, They were a lot cheaper, too.

## Village year

The year of an English village was measured in two ways: by the seasons and by the Christian saints' days and festivals. After the thanksgiving of the Harvest Home supper, there was a brief lull before the process would start again. Once a new workforce had been engaged at the 'hiring fair', the task of clearing and preparing the fields for the next year's planting would get underway. For sheep farmers, there would be a tense time in the New Year when lambs were on the way, but afterwards they could relax until shearing in midsummer. At around this time, the first hay would be cut, and then, in late August, the skies would be watched carefully as it became time to reap the main harvest once more.

Meanwhile, the old pagan calendar of fertility rites and thanksgiving ceremonies had been superceded (officially at least) by Christian celebrations such as Easter and Christmas. For most people, the festivities merely involved a few days without work, but as this could also mean a few days without pay, they were not always a cause for rejoicing. In many villages, local traditions developed from obscure pagan origins; their ritual significance forgotten, they simply provided the excuse for energetic horseplay and an opportunity to let off some steam.

## The quintessential village

It is rare to find a village that can boast every one of the physical characteristics mentioned at the beginning of this Introduction, and the few villages that do possess all these attributes do not necessarily represent the epitome of the English village. Much has to do with the way in which the various elements interrelate, with a significant part of a village's character coming from the nature of the spaces in between. The search for the quintessential village becomes that much more daunting when you realize that every village is in fact unique.

# The South and South

*One of England's oldest regions in terms of settlement, the landscape of the south has altered much over time. Along its northern seaboard, erosion has edged the shore towards villages that formerly lay inland, while in the south, deposition has silted up ports and estuaries, stranding coastal settlements several kilometres from the sea. The eerie flatlands of the Romney marshes are largely the result of artificial drainage while the once-impenetrable Forest of the Weald has been transformed by human*

# East

activity; vast stretches of woodland being cleared to make way for farmland and settlements, as well as to provide timber for construction and fuel for early industry.

Throughout most of southern England, a lack of local building stone encouraged the widespread fabrication of timber-framed buildings. Distinctive weatherboarded houses can be found in Wealden Surrey, Sussex and Kent (also an area of decorative tile hanging), while the clays of Hampshire supported brick-making. In the chalklands the main construction materials were flint and clunch (a soft limestone). Only in the north-west, at the edge of the limestone belt, was stone widely used.

A long coastline has meant that untold numbers of travellers, settlers, invaders and traders have caught their first glimpse of England here. As a result, the south has been subject to the shaping influence of so many peoples, cultures and traditions that a representative type of village probably does not exist.

LEFT: *The River Cuckmere curves gracefully around the village of Alfriston in East Sussex, to eventually meet the sea at Exceat. In the days when England's roads were barely formed its rivers provided vital communications and transportation links between settlements.*

# CHILHAM
## KENT

 hilltop stronghold since ancient times, Chilham is said to be the place where the Britons made their last stand against the Roman invaders, pushing back the tenth legion and killing one of Caesar's captains, Julius Laberius, in the process. Local legend has it that his grave was cut into a 45-metre (150-foot) Neolithic long barrow, which lies about a kilometre (½ mile) to the south-east of the village; a place known to this day as Julieberries Graves. Ultimately victorious, it seems that the Romans took advantage of the excellent strategic position afforded by the small hill in the valley of the River Stour upon which Chilham now stands, for possible Roman foundations have been identified beneath the walls of the village's curtain-walled octagonal Norman keep.

'Cilleham' was first recorded half a century before its entry was written in the Domesday survey of 1086. Gradually this earlier version of Chilham village developed and grew around the gate of the imposing Norman fortress, to which the villagers would have provided food and services while enjoying a measure of protection in return. However, the present-day Chilham Castle is, in fact, a fine Jacobean mansion completed in 1616. Often attributed to Inigo Jones, and landscaped by John Tradescant, it was built for Sir Dudley Digges. An Oxford-educated judge and MP, Digges became an important official at the court of James I. He was also a 'Virginia Adventurer', investing his money in the commercial colonization of America; his son, who later became Governor of Virginia, is credited with having introduced the silk-worm there, using cuttings from mulberry trees on the Chilham Estate, which he had planted on Mulberry Island.

Chilham Castle stretches along the north side of the village square, while facing it from the south is the mainly 15th-century church of St Mary (once also used as a school). For all its decorative flint- and stone-work the church now finds itself peering out from behind the 16th-century White Horse pub. Rows of attractive black-and-white half-timbered houses and shops stand either side of the square: a treasure trove of wonderful architectural detail that repays closer inspection. Nearly all of these buildings are medieval in origin, although some have been refaced in brick and so look much younger.

A steep, winding lane descends from each of the square's four corners; all have their own character and appeal, although only High Street can boast shops and a wonderful leaning Wealden house. At the bottom of the hill stands a 15th-century inn, the Woolpack, complete with heavy, dark beams, inglenook fireplaces and, of course, a ghost or two.

The only blot on this otherwise unspoilt view of Old England is the car park in the middle of the square, its tarmac covering what was once the village green. There is just one day every year – Spring Bank Holiday Monday – when vehicles are banished. Then the villagers reclaim the area for their Pilgrim's Fair, commemorating the time long ago when Chilham was on the Pilgrim's Way from Winchester to Canterbury. Market stalls are erected; the villagers don medieval costume and the whole place slips back into the past, as the square becomes once more the province of people.

*RIGHT: Taylor's Hill, one of four lanes leading from Chilham's medieval market square. Chilham is thought to mean 'village of a person named Cilla' but may refer to a local stream (or 'cille' in Old English).*

# SMARDEN

## KENT

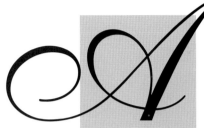n ancient oak forest once covered much of Kent and Sussex. It was known as the Forest of Anderida, or Andreswald, from which the name Weald is derived. Over time, and with much effort, small clearings or 'dens' were carved from the dense woodland. Pigs would be put to graze on the acorns that fell in and around these open areas: gradually, trees gave way to downland and pasture. It was a slow process, but eventually the plain was dotted with small settlements connected by waterways or a few hard-won roads and tracks.

First recorded in the early 12th century, Smeredaenne – later Smarden – was one such settlement; its Old English name meaning 'butter-producing woodland pasture'. A hundred years later Adam de Essex was recorded as rector of Smarden, and by the end of that century the Bell Inn had already become a popular halt on the old pilgrims' road from Winchester to Canterbury that passed to the north-west of the village. The Bell still attracts visitors today, but Adam's church has made way for a building so impressive in its scale that it has been dubbed the 'Barn of Kent'. St Michael's is a masterpiece of early medieval construction. Built during the first half of the 14th century, it stands as testament to Smarden's success as a leading Wealden wool town.

*BELOW: Many of Smarden's fine timber-framed houses were built during the prosperous times of the 15th and 16th centuries.*

Encouraged by Edward III, Flemish craftsmen settled in the area to manufacture broadcloth and to pass on their skills to the English weavers. In Smarden, as elsewhere, the newcomers were accommodated in fine new properties such as the Dragon House in the main street, constructed for the Pell family in 1331. So impressed was the king by the success of his initiative that in 1333 he granted Smarden a weekly market and annual fair, thereby transforming the village into a town.

During Smarden's heyday in the 14th and 15th centuries, many more substantial properties began to fill the gaps in this previously scattered settlement. Chessenden, built in The Street in 1462, is a typical Wealden hall house. Formerly called Smarden House, it has served the village over the years as a poor house and village hall. Cloth Hall, built several decades earlier in Water Lane as a yeoman's farmhouse, eventually became a wool warehouse where the local broadcloth was both stored and sold. But later, as the Industrial Revolution gathered pace, the local 'cottage' cloth industry was forced into inevitable decline. The introduction of hops and oasts in the mid-19th century went some way towards softening the blow, but today Smarden is a village once more.

Winner of Kent's 'Best Kept Village' award on several occasions, Smarden, set on a tributary of the River Medway known as the Beult, is today a delightful mix of white Kentish weatherboarding and aged half-timbering. The old butcher's shop survives, as do the post office and village pump; and while the school, founded by Stephen Dadson in 1720, moved to new premises in 1864, the Old School House still stands. There are two public houses in the centre of the village: the Flying Horse (probably named for a local racecourse long since closed) and the Chequers, reputedly haunted by the ghost of an old soldier murdered there for his purse. Just around the corner in Water Lane, Mathew Hartnup's House displays the rhinoceros of the Apothecaries' Company, indicating that it was once the

home of a physician. The main part of the house dates from the late 15th century with an eastern extension dated 1672. Now and then the deceptively placid Beult will overrun its banks, but villagers no longer need to resort to the use of a ferry along Water Lane, as pumps were installed in 1990. Having discovered how to keep the waters at bay, Smarden is no doubt looking for a way to retard the passage of time. Yet for now it remains one of Kent's loveliest old villages.

*ABOVE: The hops picked in the fields around the village would be taken to be dried in an oast house such as this one.*

# ALFRISTON

## EAST SUSSEX

There is a broad green valley in the South Downs through which meanders the lovely River Cuckmere. Five kilometres (three miles) from the sea, there is a kink in the river's course, a peaceful place where in prehistoric times a track (known today as the South Downs Way) crossed its leisurely flow by means of a ford. It was here that the Saxon Ælfric settled with his people and developed a substantial village on the gentle slopes above the sparkling curve of water. 'Ælfric's Tun' was recorded as Alvricestone by the Domesday commissioners, and the name knew several variations before becoming Alfriston.

The village's great 14th-century flint and greensand church is a replacement for an earlier wooden structure that once housed the bones of a Saxon saint. We are told that foundation stones laid on ground at the western edge of Alfriston, continually went missing, only to be discovered later on the opposite side of the village in the field known as the Tye. Many believed it to be the work of God, while others swore it was the Devil's doing. Progress on the new church stalled while the argument raged. Then, one day four pure white oxen were seen to lie down on the Tye, their bodies forming a perfectly symmetrical cross, and so, apparently, the matter was settled.

The Tye is also the location for the first property purchased by The National Trust. In 1896, it paid £10 for a derelict oak-framed open-hall house. Now fully restored, Alfriston's 'Clergy House', once occupied by the rector, is a unique example of a small double-ended yeoman's residence, or farmhouse, with shaped oak timbers, infill panels of lath and daub and a traditional Kentish chalk floor sealed with sour milk.

There is a wealth of vernacular architecture in Alfriston, much of it timber framed and crooked beneath roofs of glorious Horsham slate, although many elderly buildings can only support these heavy stone tiles at the eaves. Two ancient inns both built around 13th century cores almost face each other across the narrow high street. The magnificent George Inn has been continuously licensed since 1397, while the Star Inn was once the 'Starre of Bethlehem'. Until the 16th century it was maintained by the monks of Battle Abbey as a hostel for friars and pilgrims travelling to and from the shrine of St Richard at Chichester.

So often has the 15th-century market cross been knocked down by traffic that now only a stump of the original remains. Alfriston enjoyed four centuries as a market town, but the departure of soldiers stationed there during the Napoleonic wars precipitated a serious downturn in its fortunes. As the local economy failed, the looting and smuggling that had been going on unobtrusively for many years, along the coast and up the River Cuckmere, became big business. Stanton Collins, owner of the Market Cross Inn (later renamed Ye Old Smugglers Inn), led the infamous Alfriston gang. His inn's 21 rooms, 47 doors, 6 staircases and multitude of hiding places made a perfect base; it was almost as though it had been built with thwarting excise men in mind!

These days it is a romanticized version of smuggling that is celebrated in places such as Moonraker's restaurant. Tea rooms, gift shops and antique shops have replaced the tallow chandlers and glove makers, but the inns still do good business for Alfriston has become one of the most visited villages in East Sussex.

*RIGHT: The jettied first floor of the elaborately carved Star Inn shelters a startling red-painted figurehead in the form of a highly stylized lion, 'rescued' from a Dutch ship wrecked in the English Channel in the late 17th century.*

# AMBERLEY
## WEST SUSSEX

**R**esting on a low ridge at the foot of the rolling South Downs, Amberley is a perfectly preserved miscellany of old building styles and materials all sheltering in romantic fashion beneath the massive walls of a ruined castle. To the south, sheep trim the grassland around Amberley Mount, while to the north a broad, flat sweep of protected wetlands on the flood plain of the River Arun, known as Amberley Wild Brooks, supports a rich diversity of flora and fauna. Amberley's proximity to the longest river in Sussex has not always been a source of fascination and delight, however. Before the introduction of sluices to control the water level, the village experienced regular flooding.

A path from the Wild Brooks leads you past the Norman church of St Michael, which is pressed up against the towering ruins of Amberley Castle. Beneath a high roof supported by massive stone pillars, fading medieval frescoes enliven an otherwise ascetic interior, while outside blackberries ripen among the gravestones in the leaf-dappled sunshine.

In the 13th century, a manor house was built behind the church as a summer palace for the Bishops of Chichester; its castle-like curtain wall being added in 1377 when, to protect his new great hall against possible attack by the French, Bishop Reede decided fortifications were required. The castle's defences were not to be tested for more than 250 years, and then by not French troops but English, for Amberley was a Royalist stronghold during the English Civil Wars; its great 14th-century battlements eventually succumbing to the forces of Parliament. Today, Amberley Castle is an award-winning family-run hotel.

Although the castle has dominated the surrounding landscape for more than 600 years, its presence is hardly felt within the little village, whose delightful old houses and cottages seem to incorporate every type of building material found in this region. Any hard edges are softened by an abundance of creeping, climbing and trailing vegetation that springs forth from delightful flower gardens. Amberley is sometimes called the 'Pearl of Sussex', and it is little wonder that it was once home to no fewer than 15 artists' studios, the most famous occupant of which was Edward Stott, who lived in the village from 1885 until his death in 1918.

Set among water meadows, farms and cider apple orchards, and close to a river celebrated for its good fishing, Amberley is truly a picture-book village, so few now would suspect its industrial past. Chalk had long been quarried from pits in the hillside, but by 1840 several lime producers were working on a site beside the main road, the winding smoke from their many kilns visible for miles around. Amberley soon became a major centre for lime production. Initially, locally produced lime, chalk, sand and gravel (as well as hay) were taken by barge via the Arun-Wye Canal to the River Thames; later, rail transportation took over. There is still a direct link to London Victoria from Amberley Station, while the disused quarry now houses the Amberley Working Museum, its collections illustrating the industrial heritage of the region.

Amberley can boast three excellent pubs, plus a general post office and shop in which you can find delicious honey, fruit and vegetables, all produced locally. However, dwindling pupil numbers mean that the village school, although modern and well-equipped, is threatened with closure. Concerned that its loss would discourage young families from settling there, which in turn might depress the local economy and so jeopardize the future of the shop, pubs and possibly even the church, villagers have launched a vigorous campaign to save it.

# BOSHAM

## WEST SUSSEX

*S*mall the village of Bosham may be, but its name is writ large across the broad canvas of England's early history. Indeed, the chancel of the parish church features in the Bayeux Tapestry as the place where King Harold prayed before his unfortunate excursion across the English Channel in 1064 and a map that accompanies the Anglo-Saxon Chronicle includes Bosham among the handful of places identified.

Occupying a small peninsula that pushes into a tidal creek at the eastern end of Chichester Harbour, Bosham (pronounced Bozzum) is now a peaceful haven for yachts and small pleasure craft. When the tide is out, the village is stranded at the edge of vast mudflats upon which gulls and wading birds abound. And yet steep flights of steps leading to elevated front doors along the quayside should give sufficient warning that at other times the water can rise high enough to completely submerge any unwisely parked car.

Today, there is no through route, but in Roman times the village was a busy port. Then in the 7th century, an Irish monk called Dicul led a small monastic community at Bosanhamm (or 'the watermeadow of Bosa'); his church, built on the site of a Roman Basilica, becoming the focal point of an important ecclesiastical centre. Yet when Harold attended mass here in his local church, the structure within which he knelt would have been relatively new. Dedicated to the Holy Trinity, its earliest parts can be dated to the reign of King Cnut (or Canute), who had a palace here and who is said to have chosen the tidal waters of Bosham harbour to illustrate the limited extent of his powers. Today Holy Trinity's proud spire rises above Quay Meadow (a village green in all but name) and the tiled rooftops of the small brick and flint fishermen's cottages that crowd the foreshore.

Over the years several sets of unidentified human remains have been uncovered within Bosham's church but whether they are indeed the bones of Cnut's eight-year-old daughter (reputed to have drowned in the nearby millstream), Herbert of Bosham (Thomas à Becket's secretary and witness to his murder), Earl Godwin and even his son, King Harold himself, may never be known. Given its antiquity and historic location it is unsurprising that many colourful stories have attached themselves to this ancient church. One such is the tale of a tenor bell stolen by raiders in the time of Cnut, but lost by them in the bay. It is said that the bell still rings out from beneath the waves, in unison with those in the church tower.

Until the early 20th century, the economy of the village was based largely on oysters, dredged up along the coast of France or in the Solent and then grown-on in beds running the entire length of the waterfront. The quayside was busy with fishing boats, schooners and barges, supplied and maintained by local shipyards and for a while, Bosham was the second largest oyster-producing centre in England; but the industry declined after the First World War when limpets wiped out the oyster beds, although recently there has been something of a revival. Yet the fame of Bosham's fishermen rests on a centuries-old act of kindness. When, in 1664, a plague scare led to the city of Chichester's gates being sealed, only the fresh fish delivered by boats from Bosham saved the beleaguered citizens from starvation.

*RIGHT: Bosham's busy harbour saw the arrival and departure of many Saxon kings and Earls. William of Normandy seized the estate after the Conquest, its church being assessed in 1086 as one of the wealthiest in England.*

# CHIDDINGFOLD

## SURREY

To this day, the village of Chiddingfold remains a settlement in a woodland clearing, as the final element of its name suggests. Unsurprisingly, the surrounding forest has played an important role in the village's history. Long the source of fuel for the region's iron foundries, the 13th century saw a new industry emerge that exploited the locally available charcoal and sand, as glass foundries lit up to the south of the village. Soon men such as Lawrence Vitrarius, or 'Lawrence the glassmaker', were producing vessel and window glass of such high quality that its fame spread throughout Europe. There is Chiddingfold glass in St Stephen's Chapel, Westminster, and St George's Chapel at Windsor, but – surprisingly – very little in the village itself. More than 400 fragments collected from foundry sites around the village make up just one small lancet window in the church.

Under the influence of craftsmen from Germany and France, and later Huguenot refugees in the middle of the 16th century, the industry grew in both output and sophistication. However, the process required large quantities of charcoal, and the

*OPPOSITE: At one time this pretty village duck pond would have been a vital source of drinking water for the livestock that grazed the nearby green.*

*BELOW: St Mary's church was built in the 13th century, but previously there may have been a wooden church on this site from as early as the 10th century.*

number of suitable trees was dwindling fast. Competition for fuel between the glass and iron foundries was fierce until, in 1615, a Royal Proclamation prohibited the use of charcoal in glass production. The chronicler Aubrey states that some villagers, perhaps resenting the foreign glass-masters, had declared their foundries a nuisance, although the official reason for the local industry's suppression was that oak and iron were vital to the maintenance of the English fleet, while glass was not.

Yet the prosperity that sprang from the foundries is clearly visible in the fine brick and half-timbered properties that line the eastern edge of the village green. Some of them may have stood there for 600 years or more, although several have acquired new facades as building fashions have changed. One that has recently reverted to its former appearance is the Crown Inn, which had its covering of hanging tiles removed in 1951, revealing a wonderful timbered exterior. Possibly built as early as 1258, it is Surrey's oldest licensed house, having been an inn from the end of the 14th century.

Once merely an unmade forest lane, the now busy A283 separates St Mary's Church and the attractive duck pond nearby from a village green so vast that when the young Edward VI stayed at the Crown, his 4,000-strong retinue made camp there. Chiddingfold's furnaces may have been extinguished long ago, but the village has since become famous for fire of a different kind. For the past 150 years or more an annual bonfire and fireworks party has been held on the nearest Saturday to the 5th of November, Guy Fawkes Night, when the green plays host to thousands of visitors once again.

# GODSTONE

## SURREY

The small hamlet of Church Town, Godstone, is close to perfection. A simply stunning assemblage of the truly old and the artfully antique, it is a tiny corner of Old England tucked away down an almost hidden country lane. Birdsong, and the tolling of a solitary chapel bell are virtually the only sounds in a place where time seems to stand still – a spell broken only by the occasionally audible distant din of traffic.

Looking centuries older than their 132 years, St Mary's Almshouses, by local architect Sir George Gilbert Scott, are so special that one is inclined to forgive his trespasses against the ancient Norman church of St Nicholas next door, of which his 1873 'restoration' left barely a trace. The eight compact almshouses that crowd around a pretty courtyard with a well at its centre have their own chapel dedicated to Mabel Fanny Hunt (built as a mother's memorial to her young daughter) its walls delightfully timbered and decorated. But if it is real age you are seeking, you have only to cross the lane to find the splendid 300-year-old Potter's Cottage, while a little further on stands the old Pack House, a former coaching inn dating from the 1400s.

If you can tear yourself away from this oasis of tranquility, a walk of about 800m (½ mile) along Bay Path will bring you past the old 'Town Pond' (now a nature reserve) into the heart of the village of Godstone. Dating from about AD 950, the settlement appears in Domesday under the name of Wachelstede. However, it is said that at the end of the first millennium, king Ethelred II's daughter Goda had owned a farm (or 'tun') close by, the name 'Goda's Tun' eventually supplanting that of Walkinstead, and finally being corrupted into Godstone.

The village lies in a gap in the North Downs. Here the slopes were once planted with fragrant hops and a fine post mill stood where now only foundations are faintly visible. Stone and silver sand were mined near here, and in Elizabethan times leather working was important. But for centuries the main industry of this area was iron. Godstone's many ponds were created by dams, known locally as bays, which supplied the power to drive the powerful hammers. Even so, greater wealth came from the gunpowder mills of the Evelyn family. Leigh Mill to the south of the village became one of several in the area whose stones were used to mix sulphur, charcoal and saltpetre. Sir John Evelyn and his wife have memorial effigies in St Nicholas's Church, and a visit to the tomb is recorded by his better-known kinsman, the diarist John Evelyn, in the 17th century.

Today the village has a wide high street of attractive shops plus an expansive green with a delightful pond in one corner – one of seven in the vicinity. Nearby stands The White Hart Inn, a timbered building from the Tudor period, whose orderly flower garden so impressed William Cobbett that he gave Godstone a glowing review in his famously critical *Rural Rides* (1830). The inn also claims the past patronage of two queens – Elizabeth I and Victoria – as well as a Russian tsar.

Being situated at the junction of two main roads – the A25 and the A22 – and less than 2km (1.2 miles) from London's massive ring road (the M25) modern development at Godstone was inevitable. Happily, the 20th-century houses are grouped discretely around the periphery of the old village centre and Godstone has lost little of its historic charm and character.

# EAST GARSTON

## BERKSHIRE

*I*n recent times the Lambourn Valley has become known as the 'Valley of the Racehorse'; the springy turf of the open chalk downs making ideal gallops upon which horses can be trained. In this respect, it seems that at least one aspect of life here has stayed the same for almost 1,000 years for during the reign of Edward the Confessor (1042-66), a local landowner named Esgar was the king's 'staller' or 'count of the stable' – a possible origin for the word 'constable'. It is thought that his particular area of responsibility was as master of the royal stud.

The Domesday Book records that one of Esgar's many estates was known as Esgar's 'tun', or farmstead. By the 19th century, the settlement's local pronunciation of 'Argasson' had somehow evolved into 'East Garston', which explains why there is no West Garston to be found nearby, since the village's name has nothing at all to do with its geographical location. Some say that it was Esgar, in his capacity as Sheriff of Middlesex, who surrendered London to William at the Norman Conquest. However, the Domesday commissioners mention only the surrender of his estates to Geoffrey de Mandeville.

There were two mills at East Garston in de Mandeville's time, for it would appear that the river Lambourn that today flows languidly through the village was much more energetic in centuries past. Its waters have now diminished to the extent that they disappear completely for much of the year, yet whether crossing a picturesque stream or merely a wide ditch, East Garston's charming little bridges remain. No doubt in early times this precious (and probably more reliable) source of water, together with the light soil found in these parts, held great appeal for potential set-tlers. Ancient earthworks and artefacts found in the vicinity indicate that this area has been occupied almost continuously since the end of the last Ice Age.

Much later, from the mid-14th century, when sheep grazed the downs and the nearby town of Newbury became famous for its wool and cloth, East Garston's yeomen farmers profited from this expanding market. Their descendants became wealthy enough to build sturdy, timber-framed houses, several of which survive, although many of the buildings have warped and bowed over time. Lovingly cared for by their present custodians, the dwellings endure with a tenacious beauty under roofs of weathered, moss-covered tiles or heavy 'wigs' of sweeping thatch that almost touch the ground.

Undeniably lovely, East Garston is far more than an appealing collection of picture-book cottages beside a pleasant stream. The villagers, who number under 600 in all, hold an annual fête and have a fast-growing social club – they form a small and friendly rural community that takes great pride in its beautiful surroundings. Nor could it be said that East Garston rests solely on past achievements. Its Pound Farm became a well-known training yard for racehorses more than a century ago: today the village is home to no fewer than three excellent stables. This is a place that has its roots securely in the past, while keeping its sights firmly on the future. One indication that East Garston is determined to move with the times is that now the villagers are able to order groceries from the village store via the internet!

*RIGHT: Thatched timber-framed cottages form a hap-hazard line along the banks of the River Lambourn, their small gardens tumbling down to the water's edge. Several of East Garston's picturesque dwellings date from the late 16th century.*

# HAMBLEDEN

## BUCKINGHAMSHIRE

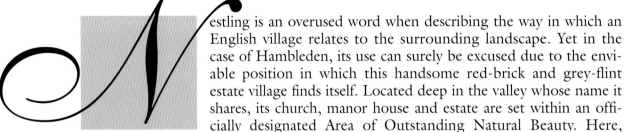estling is an overused word when describing the way in which an English village relates to the surrounding landscape. Yet in the case of Hambleden, its use can surely be excused due to the enviable position in which this handsome red-brick and grey-flint estate village finds itself. Located deep in the valley whose name it shares, its church, manor house and estate are set within an officially designated Area of Outstanding Natural Beauty. Here, against a delightful backdrop of wooded hills, uniformity of material and style does not become monotonous. Instead, subtle variations in form and arrangement have created a captivating harmony safeguarded today by a National Trust preservation order.

Viewed individually the majority of Hambleden's neat houses and cottages are architecturally unremarkable, yet the whole is most definitely greater than the sum of its parts; and while its buildings would appear to be largely of the same age, closer inspection reveals that the fabric of this handsome village spans the last four centuries. But

Hambleden's origins are far older: the Domesday Book records an already well-established community.

There was a Norman church here in 1218 when the infant Thomas de Cantelupe was baptized, probably at the same font that serves in the church to this day. In 1320 this remarkable son of Hambleden, cleric, reformer and close friend of Simon de Montfort, became the last Englishman to be canonized. Perhaps this was the catalyst that brought about the rebuilding of the church that century.

The early 17th century saw a new manor house built upon the site of the saint's birthplace. In April 1646, Charles I took refuge there overnight during his flight from Oxford to St Albans, and in October 1797, James Thomas Brudenell was born there. Better known as the seventh Earl of Cardigan, he was the English lieutenant-general that led the ill-advised 'Charge of the Light Brigade' in 1854. Today, the estate is in the hands of the Smith family, having been purchased a century and a half ago by William Henry Smith, who made such a success of the newsagents business founded by his father.

There is no longer a weekly market in Hambleden; essentials can be purchased at the combined village store and post office. Tucked away down a side road, the Stag and Huntsman retains the authentic atmosphere and intimate rooms of a traditional country pub. Meanwhile, the village green has shrunk to such a degree that it is now merely a patch of grass around the base of a chestnut tree on a small triangular island, with the village pump squeezed into one cobble-stoned corner. As recently as 50 years ago, this was still the main source of water for the village.

# TURVILLE

## BUCKINGHAMSHIRE

*I*n AD 796, the great Saxon warrior Offa had been king of Mercia for nearly 40 years. It was 17 years since he had defeated the West Saxons at Benson, and three since he had founded the Benedictine monastery at St Albans. Old and battle weary, he died that year and was succeeded by his son, Ecgfrith, who, during his short 20-week reign, found time to gift to the abbey at St Albans the 'dry open land', or 'thyrefeld', that lay at the head of the Hambleden Valley only a stone's throw from the site of his father's famous victory.

Turville has always been a small village of small houses dwarfed by the surrounding Chiltern Hills. A ditch skirting the vicarage garden is perhaps evidence of just one of the many minor Norman encampments known to have existed in the area, for great numbers of Saxons refused to accept conquest by William and waged a form of guerilla warfare from the thick forests of beech nearby. In fact, outlaws hiding out in the dense woodland remained a problem for centuries until a Steward of the Chiltern Hundreds was appointed to get the situation under control. Much later, during the Second World War, the same trees provided cover for a black market in undeclared livestock.

*RIGHT: There are only 32 dwellings in Turville with much of the architecture dating from the 16th century.*

Even so, the charming scene of timbered cottages with sagging walls and jumbled brick infill, slumbering by the side of a tiny green, all under the watchful eye of an ancient squat-towered church, gives no hint that life here has ever been anything but tranquil. But at the turn of the last century, under the floor of that very church, the skeletal remains of a woman were uncovered in a great stone coffin whose only legitimate occupant should have been a 13th-century priest. Two holes in her skull, combined with her unorthodox resting place, led many to suspect foul play, albeit several hundred years in the past.

St Mary's is indirectly responsible for the licensing of Turville's only pub, which is located in an impressive black-and-white half-timbered house. Built in the year 1550, it was forced to become a tavern in 1617, apparently in response to a group of truculent builders working on the church, who threatened to strike unless provided with satisfactory victuals. Its name, the Bull and Butcher, is said to derive from the phrase the 'Bullen butcher', which refers to Henry VIII's unpopular solution to the inconvenience of his marriage to Anne Boleyn, although the pub sign hanging outside depicts a more literal interpretation. Today, the pub retains many of its old features, including original floor tiles, heavy oak beams, an inglenook fireplace and, surprisingly, a 15-metre (50-foot) well in the appropriately named 'Well Bar'. In addition, this lovely 16th-century building is said to have a 20th-century ghost, a former wartime landlord who died in tragic circumstances.

In the 18th century chair making was an important craft in the Chilterns. Legs for the chairs were crafted from the plentiful local beechwood by men known as 'bodgers' who often worked within the forest although, unsurprisingly, the front yard of the Bull and Butcher was another preferred location. There were 'bodgers' in Turville as recently as the 1930s.

Turville has a good number of fascinating old buildings, but perhaps the one that draws the most visitors is not actually *in* the village at all. It is the

enchanting black-capped weatherboarded smock mill, which stands in lofty solitude high upon a ridge behind the creeper-clad cottages, and famous for its supporting role in the film *Chitty Chitty Bang Bang*. Not to be outdone, the village itself has since played host to its fair share of film crews. It is not unusual these days to find on the pub's excellent menu several dishes whimsically named for various television and film productions, alongside the 'Chitty Chitty Bangers and Mash'.

*ABOVE: A traditional English pub, the 16th century Bull and Butcher is located within a conservation area of Outstanding Natural Beauty.*

# GREAT MILTON

## OXON

*U*ntil canals and railways made the transportation of materials for small-scale building projects feasible, most dwellings were constructed from whatever could be gathered, hewn, dug or quarried in the immediate vicinity. In the case of Great Milton, this meant limestone. It was used in large dressed blocks or as coarse rubble walling, the latter sometimes disguised by colour-washing; quarries in the village itself providing much of the necessary raw material. However, in 1864, the completion of a new railway connection at nearby Thame finally made it possible to import bricks, tiles and stone from further afield.

Situated in the oldest part of the settlement, the fine church of St Mary the Virgin can boast features dating from the 13th century. In the days before there was a church organ, music would have been provided by a group of villagers playing various instruments and here, preserved in a glass case can be found an ophicleide (a bass brass instrument), key-bugle, concertina and cello.

Adjacent to the churchyard, the manor house (largely 15th-century with 17th-century extensions) is now an internationally known country hotel and restaurant. While nearby, in the area known as Church End, an impressive assortment of Tudor buildings can be found. They include, rather unusually, two former prebendal farms (a prebend was a property awarded to a priest to provide his stipend, or income) and the Priory, which is often erroneously reported as the home of John Milton. Although the great poet undoubtedly stayed there on occasion, it would have been as the guest of John Thurloe, Secretary of State to Oliver Cromwell (another frequent visitor). But perhaps the most interesting dwelling is the unassuming Harrington House. This much-altered building, seemingly mid-16th century in date, could well conceal a core from three centuries earlier. A well in the cellar provided water for the property, which might once have been the priest's house.

There is, in fact, rather a lot of water in Great Milton, although little is visible at first glance. A stream emerges from nearby woodland and then passes beneath the road not far from Church End. Reliable throughout the year, it was a convenient filling stop for the many steam-powered traction engines that passed that way. All around the village, springs bubble to the surface, while tiny underground streams running only a couple of metres or so beneath ground level frequently emerge in cottage gardens. There were also several public wells in the village and a pond, to the north of the triangular village green, the latter being filled in shortly after the First World War when new houses were built.

By the 16th century, the focus of Great Milton's farming community had shifted away from Church End and was concentrated along a ridge to the north, near the common land. There is a subtle linear transition in building materials from south to north as the buildings get younger, while another sign of change can be seen in the number of residential properties whose former function is recalled in their name. They include: the Old Red Lion; the Bell House (formerly the Bell inn); King's Head House (another former public house); the Old Vicarage; the Old Stores (the village shop for more than 100 years); the Old Schoolhouse (16th-century, with a later extension); the Saddlery; and the Old Forge.

*RIGHT: Priory Bank cottages were built in the early 18th-century. Stone quarried from the nearby Priory estate forms the outer walls of this picturesque row of four thatched farm-labourers cottages while some of the interior walls are wattle and daub.*

# GREAT TEW
## OXON

BELOW: *Great Tew's decorative ironstone cottages sit beneath roofs of Cotswold tiles or neatly shaped thatch.*

D usk falls early on the green at Great Tew. The tall trees at its edge throw deep shadows across the soft grassy mounds and the small lamps that glow warmly on the 16th-century inn provide the only illumination. The Falkland Arms nestles at the end of a line of delightful thatched cottages, one of which is also a quaint village shop; facing them, the neat Victorian school can be glimpsed only faintly in the twilight. The scene is an inviting one at all times of the day, which is as it was intended, for many men laboured long and hard to create it.

In 1819, having already embarked on an ambitious plan to reshape his estate at Great Tew, M. R. Boulton, turned his attention to the village. Under the guidance of architect Thomas Rickman, the project progressed throughout the 1820s. Cottages gained decorative stone porches and other ornamental details. Small attractive gardens with quickset hedges were arranged at their doorsteps, while more practical plots of a quarter of an acre were laid out behind. Roads were closed and re-routed, hedges dug out, ornamental trees planted, and outhouses were converted into dwellings, filling in the spaces between existing rows of cottages. Later, many of the tiled roofs were replaced with thatch. Boulton took an active role in the scheme and work continued right up until his death in 1842.

Yet even though its rustic charms have been exaggerated to a point just short of caricature, at its heart Great Tew remains an ancient place. Formerly known as Cyrictiwa, or 'Church Tew', it was an important ecclesiastical centre connected with other villages in the large parish by a network of lanes and ancient trackways branching from its centre. On a ridge above the village stands the church, its interior walls adorned with exceptional 13th-century paintings of the Passion Cycle that must have shone with a colourful brilliance when new. But there was a church here before Domesday, and even before that there is evidence of human habitation in the area stretching back to prehistoric times.

The Saxon settlers who chose this spot on the north slope of a valley well watered by spring-fed streams may have

carried on where the Romans left off: the remains of a villa only 1.5 kilometres (1 mile) away suggest that the land was already under cultivation in the 3rd and 4th centuries AD. It would later be farmed in the medieval 'open' system in four immense fields surrounding the village, although in 1341 it was reported that some of the land remained uncultivated; a situation that can only have worsened after the Black Death arrived in England in 1348. Much of the present village dates from the 16th and 17th centuries, however the later remodelling makes the buildings difficult to date.

In 1800, the Great Tew estate was much admired in the area, but a failed experiment in alternative farming methods carried out there by the innovative Scottish agriculturalist J. C. Louden forced its then owner, G. Stratton to put Great Tew up for sale in 1815, when it was bought by Boulton. By the middle of the 19th century it was a 'model' estate village, home to a community of farmers, country craftsmen and traders but over the century that followed, the fabric of Great Tew decayed to such a degree that some doubted it would survive.

Fortunately, in 1978 the Department of the Environment declared Great Tew to be of 'outstanding interest' and today the village's former unkempt appearance is but a distant memory. Derelict cottages, once as enchanting to some visitors as their immaculate counterparts, have nearly all been rescued and renovated. Its critics may complain that the village is contrived and artificial and, of course, to a degree they are right. But hopefully, the continuing popularity of this magnificent example of creative landscape management will ensure that its long-term future is secure.

# EAST MEON

## HAMPSHIRE

*S*cale the gentle chalk slope of Park Hill and you will be rewarded with a bird's-eye view of one of the most attractive villages in Hampshire. Look down upon the grand old church of St Mary, with its wonderful leaded broach spire and ornamented Norman tower, and you will instantly surmise that such exquisite craftsmanship must signify something special – and so it does.

East Meon only acquired an identity separate from that of its western counterpart in the years following the Norman Conquest, when the manor of Estmeone was granted to the monks at Winchester. The two communities previously had been ruled as a single estate of some significance, its villagers serving lords who were also kings: Alfred the Great and then, after the Conquest, William. A century later, Winchester had firmly put its stamp on this welcome acquisition in the form of grand ecclesiastical architecture, and it is likely that the men responsible for the rebuilding of Winchester Cathedral also had a hand in the parish church at East Meon.

Barely a stone's throw from the churchyard stands an imposing hall made from malmstone and flint; its walls 15m (50 ft) high and 1.5m (5 ft) thick. Developed by William of Wykeham as a hunting lodge in 1395, around a pre-Conquest core, it became the manorial court house, home to an estate management team of monks, and where successive visiting Bishops of Winchester, as lords of the manor, would dispense justice and regulate custom under the feudal system. At the beginning of the 20th century it was being used as accommodation for farm-workers, while cows found shelter in the Great Hall. Thankfully, with many original 14th-century features still intact, the house was rescued and restored in the 1920s, and is now a private residence.

Glittering like a silver-grey ribbon woven through the village, the young River Meon (whose Celtic name is thought to mean 'swift one') not only lent its name to both valley and settlement, but also once provided sufficient motive force to drive six mills. Much loved by Izaak Walton (author of *The Compleat Angler*, 1653), this defining feature of the village could be a source of despair as well as excellent trout. In 1955, its persistent flooding was finally brought under control when the river was widened and diverted, its course channelled between hard, vertical walls. Spanned in several places by bridges that are functional rather than decorative, it now resembles a tiny canal.

On 20 June 1910, fire swept through the village. Numerous fine old buildings in the vicinity of Workhouse Lane were lost; among them, two thatched cottages that from the early 1700s had served as the village workhouse, run upon the novel lines of compassion and kindness. Luckily, however, many superb houses survived. Several of which, although altered, probably date from the 14th century.

Today, East Meon is an eclectic mix of oak, plaster, brick and flint finished off with dark chocolate thatch or sober grey tiles. Yet there are flashes of colour everywhere, with panels painted in pastel shades, upper storeys of hanging red tiles, and the occasional door or window frame painted a vibrant blue. Photogenic groupings of 16th-century thatched cottages mix easily with grand brick houses from the time of William and Mary or the Georges while modern development is tucked discreetly out of sight. Beside the river, the tiny green known as Washer's Triangle is no longer draped with damp laundry. Instead, benches sit beneath young trees and contemplate the war memorial.

*RIGHT: A tamed River Meon flows through an ancient but still vital village. It has a school, combined village stores and post office and two pubs, one of which, the Izaak Walton, fittingly sits on the bank of the river.*

# LONGSTOCK

## HAMPSHIRE

$S$o often is Longstock passed over in favour of its better known neighbour, Wherwell, that perhaps it is time to do a little to redress the balance. Although only 5km (3 miles) separate the two villages, which both sit on the banks of the River Test, they could hardly be more different in character.

Wherwell feels compact and enclosed in the deep shade of a dark, tree-hung ridge. Swathes of thick, mottled thatch sweep over the tiny windows and rustic porches of timbered cream-washed cottages, while leafy lanes lead you to narrow bridges over swift water and the remnants of a 10th-century abbey. Compared with the subtle coolness of Wherwell, Longstock appears lusty and robust. Wherwell derives its name from the enigmatic Old English *hwer wella*, meaning 'cauldron spring', whereas Longstock was known as plain Stoches in the Domesday Book, which means simply 'outlying farmstead'; the 'long' was added to its name later, after the village had experienced a couple more centuries of steady growth.

OPPOSITE: *Round thatched angler's huts can be found perched on tiny islets or along the riverbank.*

BELOW: *Longstock has 41 listed buildings. Several are 16th cottages that retain their original structure and plan.*

The most picturesque approach to the village is from the north through the extensive orchards of Longstock House, once owned by John Spedan Lewis, founder of the large retail chain that bears his name. For lovers of thatch, there is plenty to enjoy at Longstock, but its dwellings are almost wholly without pretension, even sometimes a little rough around the edges, yet no less charming for their rustic honesty. With their busy farms all around and centrally located pub, the present-day custodians of Longstock have held to simple principles and maintained a relationship with the land that has been the essence of life in these parts for thousands of years. Celtic field systems have been uncovered in the parish within the shadow of the Iron Age hill fort at Danebury and the Romans, as accomplished at agriculture as they were at conquest, are known to have operated a substantial villa and farmstead in the vicinity.

But the river has also played its part in the history of Longstock. Almost 1,000 years earlier, at a time when Cnut (or Canute) was battling against Edmund Ironside, the Danes cut a 90-m (300-foot) long channel from the river, within which they built a fortified dock for the construction and maintenance of their long, flat-bottomed boats. More recently, peat was dug from the river's edge for fuel, while up until the Second World War, sedge grass cut from the banks of the Test supplied the raw materials for a cottage industry manufacturing items such as mats and baskets. Most villagers, however, worked on one of the numerous local farms or at the large corn mill, which employed more than 30 people until it closed in 1934.

# GODSHILL

## ISLE OF WIGHT

Despite the self-conscious window dressing of tea rooms, toy museums, gift shops and even a miniature village (1:10 scale), Godshill is still a wonderfully attractive place. Ignore the colourful signage and bunting, for the village seems perpetually in costume and ready to put on a show, and you will quickly come to realize that it really doesn't need to try so hard.

There is no village green to speak of, although there are some wide grass verges that often prove useful since there are precious few pavements; but the village can boast several pubs, a delightful scattering of cottages (some of warm grey stone and many with roofs of thatch), an effusion of mature, colourful gardens, and the biggest church on the Isle of Wight.

*BELOW: The classic image of Godshill. High on the summit of Church Hill and surrounded by delightful thatched greystone cottages stands the 14th century Church of All Saints. Inside is a 500-year-old wall painting depicting Christ on the Lily Cross.*

All Saints jealously guards its beautiful wall paintings and watches over its enthusiastic flock from a lofty position apparently chosen by God himself: it seems that the villagers of Godshill had similar problems to the residents of Alfriston (see page 20) when deciding where to build their place of worship. However, in this case they appear to have capitulated more readily in the face of divine intervention.

'To reach the church by way of the

steps', as the sign says, you must take the path running along one side of the curiously named Batswing Old English Tea Rooms and Gift Shop, which faces healthy competition in the sale of souvenirs from the Old Smithy nearby. There is also a handful of original 16th-century dwellings, each taking great pride in its antiquity. Since 1854, one of them has opened its doors as an enormously popular tea room. Trading under the rather grand name of Royal Essex Cottage, its popular appeal is cemented by the occasional appearance of two very charming ghosts.

About 1.5km (1 mile) to the south is the romantic, yet apparently spectre-free, shell of a Palladian mansion – Appuldurcombe House. Built in 1710 by Robert Worsley, whose family insignia is depicted on the sign of the Griffin Hotel in the village, it was abandoned only 200 years later. Then, in 1943, it was badly damaged by a landmine and most thought that the end of the story. But Appuldurcombe is currently undergoing restoration and parts are now open to the public.

Some believe Godshill to be the quintessential English village, and perhaps it appeared so, once, but now it is more accurate to call it the quintessential Isle of Wight village for Godshill seems to sum up the slightly surreal quality that pervades the whole island during the holiday season. It is as tasteful as rampant commercialism can get, and there is real quality in the attractions. The purists might choose to stay away as Godshill may not be everyone's 'cup of tea' (and tea is something that Godshill will never be short of), but there is still an old English village beneath the surface. You just have to look a bit harder to see it.

# The South West

*Renowned for its diverse and often spectacular scenery the South West of England is, moreover, an ancient landscape exhibiting traces of human occupation stretching back over many thousands of years. Since the earliest times, humankind has sought out the most sheltered spots along the region's coastline, wedged its settlements into narrow valleys or perched its dwellings precariously in tiers along their steeply sloping sides while in bolder moments, encouraged by intermittent climate changes, its*

outposts have nudged at the edges of inhospitable moors. Yet here all human endeavour remains dwarfed by the feats of those natural forces that could rend the deep cleft of a limestone gorge or thrust up a massive boss of granite.

Picturesque and dramatic; mysterious and accessible, a dazzling array of disparate settings seem to have been crammed into an absurdly compact space in this most-visited corner of England. Here you can find not only the dark granite cottages of Cornwall, with their sagging slate roofs, but also the hearty half-timbering of rural Wiltshire, the glittering flint cottages of Dorset, the warm Cotswold stone of Gloucestershire, and the rounded cob and thatch houses of Devon. Little wonder then that in the decades after the railways opened up this formerly isolated region to the less determined traveller, it quickly became the most popular holiday destination in the country.

LEFT: *A picturesque jumble of slate-roofed stone cottages and simple Georgian houses; the small fishing village of Polperro is an essential stop on any journey around Cornwall. In this region of extreme physical contrasts, there is great vernacular diversity.*

# ASHMORE

## DORSET

Ashmore means 'pool where the ash trees grow,' a name that remains appropriate to this day for the ash is still a common sight here and the large circular pool, now the village pond, also endures, although nobody seems to know quite why or how, its source being something of a mystery. It dries up temporarily, perhaps once every two decades, but for the rest of the time serves as centrepiece to the highest village in Dorset, as it has done since the Romans made their road from Badbury to Bath across this wooded hilly landscape dotted with ancient barrows. Here, the teams transporting lead from mines in the Mendip Hills to ports along the south coast would make their stop, and a Romano-British settlement grew up around the margins of their watering place.

Nearly in Wiltshire, high on a chalk summit in the Cranborne Chase at 215m (700 ft) above sea level and with spectacular panoramic views, Ashmore is today a remote farming settlement, its Roman road now little more than an overgrown path through the woods. It is hard to imagine what life here must have been like in the days before tractors and aircraft, when the snows of winter buried the lanes for weeks

*RIGHT: Attractive as well as practical, being cool in summer and warm in winter, thatch was once the most widespread of the traditional roofing methods. It requires regular maintenance and periodically almost total renewal.*

MIDDLE: *Ashmore's large pool is possibly an ancient dewpond, excavated on the othewise arid hilltop to collect rainwater, mist and dew.*

BELOW: *Home to just 150 villagers, Ashmore is a pleasant mixture of fine Georgian houses and quaint thatched cottages.*

at a time – presenting an insurmountable barrier to communications and supplies.

As with any isolated community, especially one that has survived for millennia beside a mysterious pool, a rich culture of legend and superstition has grown up in Ashmore. The focus for the Gappergennies or Gabbigammies, as the local spirits are known, appears to be an old well beneath an ash tree, called Washer's Pit. It is here, at what may once have been a holy well, that strange events are said to cluster. These range from a nearly formless apparition called simply 'It' to spine-chilling tales about various White Ladies, both corporeal and supernatural.

Throughout its history, Ashmore's main source of employment has been the manor estate. Held by the Howard family for generations, village and church have each benefited from their generosity, though try as they might almost as many generations of villagers have been unsuccessful in persuading successive squires of the need for a local pub. Instead, a new well was sunk, but at over 90m (300 feet) in depth, the task of raising a pail of water was so arduous that the villagers boycotted it, reportedly hurling the village maypole down the shaft as an expression of their dissatisfaction.

A largely agricultural settlement, there is one crop that has always proved particularly lucrative for the people of Ashmore: hazelnuts. The 'Filly Loo' is a relatively recent festival begun in the 1950s by local folk dance enthusiasts to augment the annual celebrations at the conclusion of the nutting season. Held on the Friday nearest Midsummer's Eve, Morris men and folk dancing clubs perform adaptations of traditional dances around the pond, drawing many spectators to this typically English event.

# CORFE CASTLE

## DORSET

At the northern edge of the peninsular known as the Isle of Purbeck, the massive ruins of a great Norman castle dominate the only gap in a natural barrier formed by the Purbeck Hills. While it is difficult today to see what the castle was here to defend, and against whom, it stands on the site of a timber stronghold built by a Saxon king which occupied a position once defended by Roman fortifications. The formidable 11th-century stone fortress, later to become one of five Royal castles, was extended and improved by successive kings, many of whom favoured it above all others. From here they could hunt in the Purbeck Forest while the castle's impregnable walls provided a secure repository for hoards of treasure as well as troublesome political prisoners.

Although separated by a wide natural moat, the castle and the village that grew up at its gates inevitably developed strong links yet the relationship was not the traditional one of mutual dependence. Corfe was a wealthy village in its own right and could have thrived for centuries without royal patronage. South of the settlement were numerous quarries producing the much sought-after Purbeck freestone and marble. Indeed, so prosperous

*Opposite: The imposing outline of its ruined castle still dominates the small village known originally as Corfe Gate.*

did Corfe become that in the 16th century it was incorporated as a borough returning two MPs to parliament until disenfranchised in 1832. But in time the focus of the stone trade moved to nearby Swanage, and soon afterwards Elizabeth I sold Corfe to her favourite courtier (later her Lord Chancellor) Sir Christopher Hatton. It was a double blow and by the 18th century the village's involvement in the stone trade was minimal.

In 1635, Charles I's Lord Chief Justice, Sir John Bankes, purchased the castle as a country retreat, but when Civil War broke out seven years later, Corfe, staunchly Royalist, became a prime target for the Parliamentarians. With her husband at court in London or travelling with the king, Lady Bankes was left to defend the castle against attack, assisted only by her household staff and a handful of village tradesmen. Under siege for six long weeks, the castle's massive limestone walls atop its steeply sloping mound eventually proved too much for the Roundheads. They withdrew, maintaining only a partial blockade. However, when Sir John died the following year, Colonel Bingham, the Governor of Poole, must have thought that a widow would make an easy target. Another siege ensued, with the village church doubling as the Parliamentary forces' headquarters. This time they were successful, but only through treachery when a member of the garrison within the castle, having convinced his comrades that reinforcements had arrived, opened the gates to let them in.

Most of the houses that we see at Corfe today are 18th century. These were the dwellings of stonecutters and, despite the localized decline of their industry, it seems there was no corresponding deteri-oration in their skills: many houses display the finest quality material shaped by the hands of superb craftsmen. Situated at the T-junction of Corfe's two roads and dominated by the Greyhound Hotel (two 16th-century cottages joined with stone from the castle), the little market-place with its old stone cross is surrounded by low, grey buildings, some of which retain their exterior staircases. With only the occasional modern inter-loper Corfe's old buildings squat beneath their heavy stone roofs in a pattern that has changed little for 300 years.

*Above: Many of Corfe's wonderful old buildings incorporate stone and other elements plundered from the castle, which was partially demolished by order of Parliament in 1646.*

# OKEFORD FITZPAINE

## DORSET

*D*eep in the rural heart of Dorset a small village of characterful cottages has evolved around a medieval market cross. But don't let the sleepy atmosphere fool you; there is a formidable strength of character in the people of Okeford Fitzpaine.

One of their favourite tales recounts the exploits of Robert son of Payn (or Robert Fitzpaine). He was a local landowner who, in 1264, fought with the rebel barons under Simon de Montfort, Earl of Leicester, at the Battle of Lewes. The King, Henry III, was captured but ever thinking ahead Robert decided to hedge his bets. He and another man, William Govis, purloined the royal seal and set it to a document exempting them from taxes payable on their lands - in recognition of services the two men had supposedly rendered the king at Lewes! It was a shrewd move because Henry was soon back in power but Robert had his evidence of 'loyalty' not to mention his tax free land.

*RIGHT: A winding lane lined with attractive thatched cottages leads to the 15th-century church of St Andrew in its elevated position on the south-eastern edge of the village.*

The obvious relish with which this story is told should forewarn all visitors that today's villagers are no less masters of their own destiny, although now all contracts are strictly above board. In 1966, many former tenants became the owners of their properties following the sale at auction of much of the village. The Parish Council also purchased land. Since that time, residents have campaigned successfully against speeding traffic and have ensured that all power and telephone cables are run underground. In addition, a popular refurbishment of the old village pound has recently been completed and although villagers were unable to obtain permission for a planned restoration of the 14th-century market cross, a commemorative bench was installed to mark the new Millennium instead.

Okeford Fitzpaine has retained much of its original identity, in part through the influence of the late Captain George Pitt-Rivers – the former owner of the estate, including the village – but largely due to the determination of the residents themselves. No fewer than 25 of the village's 18th-century buildings are listed, as is a 50-m (165-foot) length of raised pavement. Fragments of much older structures survive interwoven in the fabric of newer properties, and the architectural abandon with which buildings have been extended in several different styles and materials demonstrates both an individuality of spirit and an appreciation of practicality. St Lo house, for example, combines thatched timber and locally made brick with sections in flint and stone. There are several other cottages that mix flintwork and brickwork or window and door styles. One cottage near to the cross makes good use of the iron-studded oak door from the old gaol, while the churchyard wall has been partially constructed with fragments of moulded stonework from the previous church of St Andrew.

No matter that the public telephone box is steadfastly painted green in the Pitt-Rivers livery instead of the more traditional red, the community here has always been aware of the need to be flexible and to adapt to changing circumstances. Where once there were five public houses, today there is only one: the Grade II-listed Royal Oak that dates from the 19th century, while the 18th-century Bell Inn lives on as Ye Olde Bell Stores, which serves as both post office and shop. Yet Okeford Fitzpaine is not fading quietly away, nor has it become a dormitory village. New businesses are starting up alongside the traditional farms, the school is thriving and the village football team, unsurprisingly, is a force to be reckoned with.

Undeniably, things have changed in Okeford Fitzpaine: lifestyles have altered and old customs have been modified. And yet, fittingly for a community that has long recognized the intrinsic value of retaining the best from its past, a little museum sits snugly between the school and the post office, at the very heart of the village.

# DREWSTEIGNTON

## DEVON

There are two fundamental misconceptions about Drewsteignton that should be put to rest from the start. First, the village did not begin as a centre for Druids. Second, it is far more than just a convenient place to leave your car when heading off across country to Fingle's Bridge, Spinster's Rock or any of the many other delightful walks in the area. The village was Taintone in 1086, becoming Teyngton Drue in the 13th century, when Baron Dru (aka Drogo) became lord of the manor. 'The village on the River Teign belonging to a man named Drew' is the true meaning of Drewsteignton.

The writer John Timpson points out that in the 19th century many people believed the Druid theory. The reasoning behind it was this: it had been noted that several prehistoric sites were close to places with Drew in their name – Littleton Drew and Stanton Drew, for example – and therefore it seemed clear that all must have had some connection with Druidism. It was concluded that Spinster's Rock, a megalithic tomb near Drewsteignton, was actually a Druid cromlech, and so the name of the village was taken to mean 'Druid settlement by the Teign'. The New Inn in the village square was promptly renamed The Druid's Arms, yet there was a glaring flaw in this hypothesis. Careful investigation would have revealed that each of the examples named above were manors that, at some stage in their history, had been owned by the Dru (or Drewe) family, who clearly had a penchant for things prehistoric. Their name was then added to the original name of the settlement and bingo - instant druids!

Drewsteignton is a very pretty village approached through glorious scenery along steep lanes that suddenly narrow and twist. Rolling farmland gives way to a deep wooded valley as the River Teign makes its magnificent progress from Dartmoor down to the sea. Neolithic people knew the hills, the valleys and the moors here, and later the Celts and Saxons left their mark on the landscape.

The village itself sits on a peaceful hilltop at the edge of the moor. At its heart is a square around which are gathered all a villager needs to keep body and soul together: church, inn, shop and cottage.

Holy Trinity's massive walls of moorland granite were partly raised with profits from wool and tin, the main industries in the area in the 15th century. Its looming grey form dominates the small square by day, while at night its imposing tower is dramatically floodlit. The pleasantly thatched Drewe Arms pub presents a cosier aspect. In the 19th century, Drewsteignton was known for the excellence of its alehouses and it is fair to say that the tradition continues. As in so many villages these days, the shop and post office are combined into a no-nonsense little building, with the tiniest of customers' car parks at the front. Beside the Victorian village school stands the Gospel Hall, and all around are narrow lanes of pink-, white- and cream-washed cottages, most of them thatched.

Julius Drewe, founder of the Home & Colonial grocery store chain and builder of Castle Drogo (the last castle to be built in England), claimed to be descended from the ancient Dru family. His impressive granite castle, designed by Sir Edwin Lutyens, was erected about 1.5km (1 mile) to the west of Drewsteignton (1910-1930). While this seems to have gone down reasonably well with the locals, they could not resist having some fun with the man, insisting on calling his new home 'Castle Margarine' as a reference to the principal source of its funding.

A small agricultural community of fewer than 600 souls, Drewsteignton has made little concession to the holiday industry, apart from the occasional bed and breakfast. The charm of its quiet simplicity is perhaps its most attractive quality, but it gets its glad rags on once a year on Trinity Saturday, when the Teignton Fair is held in the village square.

# CLOVELLY

## DEVON

The original Clovelia of Domesday was indeed a 'cliff-top pasture,' as it's name suggests, for the earliest settlement of fisher-folk and farmers here was slightly further inland than the famously picturesque fishing village we know today, which is largely the creation of two families: the Careys and the Hamlyns.

Only pedestrians and donkeys can negotiate Clovelly's near vertical cobbled main street, whose narrow twists and turns drop you 120 metres (400 feet) in the space of less than a kilometre. And yet every day, at the height of the tourist season, up to 7,000 visitors brave the tricky descent, although far fewer manage to climb back up. In anticipation of this, a Land Rover service operates along a back road and for a small fee will return daytrippers to the comfort of their car parked outside the visitors' centre at the top of the village.

Packed tightly into a narrow combe, or valley, Clovelly's houses appear as though perched one on top of another. In almost unbroken rows, half-timbered or whitewashed cottages line the High Street, known locally as Down Along or Up Along, depending on which way you are headed, with an occasional side turning or passageway to entice the curious. Now and then you might see a sledge tied to a railing outside a cottage, the best method the villagers have of transporting their shopping

*RIGHT: Still a working fishing village. Freshly caught local lobster and crab are served in many of Clovelly's pubs, restaurants and cafes.*

*FAR RIGHT: One of many doors in the village painted in the new green livery of the Clovelly estate.*

or the suitcases of paying guests along the steep cobbled streets.

At the bottom of the hill is the steepest section of all, where the houses break rank and scatter. Here, beneath the imposing white facade of the Red Lion, which was built on the site of the fishermen's cider houses, a merry assortment of little craft crowds the slipway. Occasionally, a larger boat will tie up at the quayside as a reminder that, for all the revenue that tourism brings, Clovelly remains a working fishing village.

In the 16th century, there was a good profit to be made fishing the waters of the Bristol Channel, but too few safe harbours. So, in 1587, George Carey, Clovelly's lord of the manor, extended its diminutive 14th-century quay and added a massive stone pier. At the same time, the course of the stream running down to the harbour was diverted, the dry bed becoming a cobbled path along which donkeys would carry home the day's catch in baskets slung across their backs. The village prospered. Many of the houses we see today were built at the end of the 18th or beginning of the 19th century when Clovelly, by now in the hands of the Hamlyns, was thriving. So much so that the harbour had to be enlarged to accommodate its growing fleet of picarooners (small fishing boats) together with the ketches that brought coal and limestone for the local limekiln.

Meanwhile, the smugglers who had long operated out of Clovelly were busy making good use of the many local caves. To ensure people stayed well away from their hoards of contraband, they would spread rumours that the caves were haunted by terrible phantoms or frequented by cannibals who kept barrels of salted human flesh there!

Inspirational home of the author Charles Kingsley, who wrote both *Westward Ho!* and *The Water Babies* here, Charles Dickens was also much taken with Clovelly and both writers played a part in spreading its fame. These days, the village remains much as they would have known it, due in no small part to the efforts of the eccentric but much-loved Christine Hamlyn, who inherited the estate in 1884 and did much to preserve and enhance its character. No doubt she would be delighted that even today the trappings of tourism have been largely contained within the visitors centre, leaving the rest of Clovelly free to charm and beguile as it has done for over 200 years.

# COCKINGTON

## DEVON

The inaccessibility of Cockington's valley location, coupled with its emergence as a Victorian tourist destination at an early stage, ensured that this Domesday village was not entirely consumed by the large holiday town of Torquay, whose suburbs now surround it. However, the loss of farmland entailed in its neighbour's relentless expansion almost brought about the end of this small agricultural community. The number of farmsteads dwindled from three to one, leaving many buildings within the centre of the village empty and neglected. Hedgerows became overgrown and stone walls crumbled. Yet for all its increasing shabbiness, Cockington retained its appeal as a Torquay visitor attraction, its wild, unkempt appearance being deemed 'rustic' and 'quaint'. In distress it acquired an air of authenticity whereas its former trim appearance had smacked of artifice to some.

Yet Cockington had always been genuine. The seemingly miraculous preservation of its ancient thatched cottages, many of which can claim origins in the 14th century, was quite simply due to the estate having been in the hands of only three different families since 1066 and of one in particular, the Mallocks, lords of the manor from 1654 to 1932. Each successive holder of the title, however differently they may have viewed their relationship with their tenants, nevertheless took good care of the estate and village. From the 1930s, however, the Cockington estate had been sold and sold again and although large sections were retained as complete units, others were sold off, contributing to the steady erosion of its commercial viability and physical integrity.

Thankfully, in 1971 a crisis meeting of all the owners, tenants and other interested parties resulted in the formation of a single management board, which began to restore the village to its former glory. Cottages were renovated and redundant farm buildings were sympathetically converted into new dwellings. Grants were obtained to repair and restore the Tudor Cockington Hall while its lakes – once the fish ponds of the monks at Torre Abbey – and the gardens which surrounded them, were re-landscaped. A flock of sheep was brought in to graze the orchards where previously horses had done much damage and one hundred and fifty traditional Devon cider apple trees were planted in recognition of the fact that much of Cockington's former prosperity lay in the production of vast quantities of apples for the cider-making industry.

*RIGHT: Cockington's economy, once dependant on agriculture and horticulture, is now dominated by businesses set up to cater for the many thousands of tourists who visit each year.*

Today, visitors to Cockington Country Park, as it has been designated since 1991, can still admire the old 14th-century forge in the village centre, although sadly it is a working forge no more and the old mill, which retains its 19th-century cast iron wheel as well as the many wonderful cottages. The 16th-century gamekeeper's cottage, rebuilt following an arson attack in 1990, is now the Visitors Centre while the number of gift shops have been reduced and a tea shop opened. Tenants have all been offered new 999-year leases and hold regular meetings with the Cockington Management Advisory Board as well as local landowners. Collectively they determine and protect the future of this unique village, which is once more the 'Jewel in Torbay's Crown'.

THE
OLD
SCHOOL
HOUSE

GIFT
SHOP

At
any
time

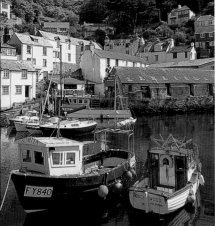

# POLPERRO

## CORNWALL

*T*iers of stone cottages, some whitewashed and others colour-washed in pastel pink or powder blue, huddle around Polperro's tiny harbour. At the point where level building space runs out, they begin to back up the steep sides of a ravine. Some cottages stand alone, while others are joined to form near-terraces, yet every property retains a unique identity, with its own idiosyncratic arrangement of windows and individual roof line. These are chunky, block-like dwellings, each of a peculiar charm, but when seen en masse, above a patchwork of shimmering reflections, the combined effect is magical.

Polperro is best seen from the water, where the simple Georgian houses around the seafront and the brightly coloured cottages picked out against the darker green background of the wooded slopes can be fully appreciated. This is the view that has adorned many a souvenir. Lobster pots and fishing nets litter the quay and small craft gently bob in the harbour, while in the outer cove beyond the sea wall, yachts are moored. At high tide, the deep drone of diesel engines can be heard above the constant screeching of the seagulls as the fishing boats return with their catch.

*RIGHT: For centuries, pilchards were the main catch for the village's many fishermen. Today thirteen commercial fishing boats operate out of Polperro; trawlers, netters, crabbers and scallopers landing a wide variety of fish and other seafood.*

There is a 'softness' here not found in similar villages on the more spectacular coast of north Cornwall. The basic form of those settlements may be similar, but along the gale-lashed Atlantic seaboard you will discover a sterner, more dramatic kind of beauty, where the sparse vegetation is wind-blasted and the trees are stunted. By contrast, Polperro's climate is so mild that the village is said to be part of the Cornish Riviera. Of course, there can be rough weather even here, and when a storm threatens the tiny mouth of the inner harbour is stopped with solid timbers slotted firmly into place.

Polperro suffers more from the landward direction. Each year, tens of thousands of holidaymakers descend (literally) onto this quaint 13th-century fishing village, and in its turn the village does its best to welcome them. The tourists come to see the Saxon bridge across the River Pol by the village green, and the retired fisherman's house decorated with countless shells, or perhaps the Elizabethan house of Dr Jonathan Couch, the fascinating 'House on Props', or the famous harbour itself.

Commercialism reaches near fever pitch in midsummer, yet in most places the disfigurement is superficial, being significantly reversed in the low season. Even so to call Polperro 'unspoilt' would be misleading, as one glance at the enormous car park will confirm. But tourism now provides the main source of income for the village, whereas once it would have been a close run thing between fishing and smuggling. In this secluded cove, the men of Polperro would unload their catch of pilchards during the day and their illicit haul of brandy and tobacco by night.

# PORT ISAAC
## CORNWALL

ort Isaac has been a fishing village for so long that it really doesn't know how to be anything else, nor would it want to be. The inevitable tourists are here, of course, and along with them the obligatory souvenir outlets and guest houses, and yet somehow Port Isaac retains a dignified air of detachment from it all.

There are prettier coastal villages, perhaps, but it has been to capture the unique atmosphere of an age-old, and essentially Cornish, fishing community that artists and poets have long flocked here. Houses from the 17th to the 19th centuries, many of them listed as of special historical importance, are packed tightly into a pleasingly irregular jumble of narrow alleys and lanes. Known locally as 'opes' and 'drangs', some of them are only 0.6 metres (2 feet) wide in places as they gradually wend their way down the steep slope to the harbour below. Everywhere can be found evidence of the passage of time: thick walls bulge, slate roofs sag and twist, and stone steps have been worn smooth and concave.

Nevertheless, this complex arrangement of many different elements has been transformed into a scene of captivating simplicity, for Port Isaac has been painted with a limited palette. Its walls are generally whitewashed, although some are left unpainted as natural stone or slate-hung, while many of its roofs are of subtly-mottled grey slate. Here and there a splash of terracotta or a spray of vibrant geraniums lift the tone.

Isaac is thought to derive from the word 'yssick', an old Cornish name for corn, and corn growing was once an important part of the village economy. But it is for fishing that Port Isaac is best known. Pilchards were the main catch here from the 16th century although cargoes of Delabole slate, stone, coal, corn, pottery and timber have all been moved across its quayside, as has the contraband of smugglers.

Today Port Isaac with its picturesque harbour, known as the Platt, is still an active fishing port, as it has been since Saxon times and the traditional character of this ancient Cornish settlement is being safeguarded for the future: its historic core has been designated a Conservation Area. It can only be hoped that, with strict planning restrictions in place and through the determined efforts of a strong resident community, Port Isaac will remain unspoilt for many years to come.

*BELOW: This narrow inlet between high cliffs has been a registered fishing port since 1338.*

# LACOCK

## WILTSHIRE

The spirit of Old England seems everywhere in Lacock. Thatched or tiled, stone-built or half-timbered, a host of medieval buildings rub shoulders with their later neighbours in a compact yet generally harmonious manner, marred only by the imposing red brick facade of the Red Lion pub, which was unhappily attached to a much older building in 1740 .

This idyllic spot close to the river Avon had been recognised as prime land for settlement by the Saxons who described their new home on the banks of the Bide Brook as 'lacuc' or 'the small stream.' It was clearly a good choice for by the time of Domesday 'Lacoc' (as it was then known) could boast, in addition to its many acres of meadows and woodland, a vineyard and two mills.

When William's great survey was produced, the village belonged to Edward of Salisbury, Sheriff of Wiltshire, and the son of one of the Conqueror's knights. In 1232, Edward's granddaughter, Ela, Countess of Salisbury, founded an abbey at Lacock in memory of her beloved late husband, William Longspee, who was the illegitimate son of Henry II. The abbey was built on Snaylesmeade meadow between the village and the River Avon, from stone quarried at Hazelbury, near Box, and oak timbers from the royal forests, including nearby Melksham.

Sometime during the following century, Lacock's magnificent stone tithe barn was erected. Constructed with cruck beams (a curved pair of timbers or 'blades', often made by splitting a suitably-shaped oak tree in half) it has a tall roof supported by a simple yet ingenious arrangement of great timbers and a broad floor of beaten earth. Here would be gathered the fleeces, hides, grain and other local produce with which the villagers, nearly all of whom were tenants of the abbey, would pay their rents and dues in addition to the labour services they were bound to perform. On a much smaller scale, although of roughly the same date, Cruck House at the west end of Church Street has one of its curved supporting end beams visible. The building no longer sports a warm roof of thatch, but this charming combination of timber, stone and brick stands as a reminder of an age when the speedy erection of a permanent dwelling could gain you the plot of land upon which it

*BELOW: Dating in part from the 13th century, King John's Hunting Lodge is Lacock's oldest inhabited building.*

stood – so long as you completed the task within one day.

Lacock's position on both the River Avon and the main cloth road from London meant that Ela's endowment of rich farmland and large sheep pastures served the village well. From the Middle Ages, the people of the village made their fortunes from wool with increasing success. Many impressive properties were constructed around a grid of four main streets, and the 15th century saw the completion of the glorious 'wool' church of St Cyriac, protected by a clever sheep gate from the beasts upon whose backs it had been built. All through the village, the weavers' cottages can be identified. Those of the 15th century have characteristic long rows of first-floor windows that lit the wide rooms needed for the newly introduced broadlooms.

A further example of Lacock's medieval prosperity can be found in the stone and timber wool merchant's house named The Sign of the Angel (after a gold coin). Built in 1480, its interior is a rich delight of original panelling, crooked walls, uneven floors, creaking stairs and low beams. Along with other substantial houses in the village, it contains a 'horse passage' giving access from the street to the stables behind. However, the honour of oldest inn in Lacock belongs to The George in West Street, which was built in 1361 formerly quite simply The Inn. As for the imposing Red Lion, situated alongside a broad High Street that was for a time the site of Lacock's busy market, it was once a farm, its modern car park taking the place of the former yard and duck pond

Early in the 18th century, a stone packhorse bridge was built beside the ford to carry Lacock's main road across the Bide Brook. At around the same time, the Blind House – a tiny, window-

less cell used as a temporary lock-up for the drunk and disorderly – was built in East Street. But as the Industrial Revolution gathered pace and the local woollen industry declined, fewer and fewer new buildings were erected. There were two notable additions, however. In the 1820s, a grand new school was constructed on the site of some old cottages; a decade later, on land near the church, a workhouse for the unemployed, destitute and sick was opened. However, work continued in the tanyard beside it, as it did in many of the local craft industries.

Meanwhile, strange magic was being worked at the abbey, or so its 13th-century founder would no doubt have thought. Following the abbey's dissolution in 1539, the building and estate – including tenancies in the village – were purchased by William Sharrington, his subsequent creative conversion of the main property mercifully retaining much of the earlier structure. The house then passed via his brother to his niece, and through her marriage it became the property of the Talbot family. John Ivory Talbot made substantial changes in the 1750s, among other things adding the large neo-Gothic entrance hall designed by Sanderson Miller.

Three generations later, the Lord of Lacock was one William Henry Fox Talbot, renowned scientist, archaeologist and pioneer photographer. In 1835, he took a photograph of a small oriel window in the abbey's South Gallery, which is the world's earliest surviving negative. Today, his achievements are celebrated in a 16th-century barn that in 1975 was converted into the Fox Talbot Photographic Museum.

These days Lacock is perhaps one of the most photographed villages in England. With its tarmac roads carefully disguised, and with no television aerials or overhead cables to break the spell, it has also become a favourite location for film and television crews making adaptations of works by writers such as Austen, Hardy and Defoe. while most recently, the abbey itself has featured in a *Harry Potter* film.

# CASTLE COMBE

## WILTSHIRE

Castle Combe is a stunning display of glorious, honey-coloured Cotswold stone, shaped by the power of medieval wool money. Often described as enchanting, its stone cottages look as though they belong in the pages of a child's story book. Perhaps 'enchanted' would be more appropriate, for Castle Combe belongs to an age that passed many centuries ago.

There was an Iron Age hillfort here before the Romans raised their own fortifications and built a villa nearby. Later, the Saxons had a stronghold in the vicinity, but it was sacked by the Danes leaving the way open for Walter de Dunstanville, great-great-grandson of Henry I, to build a Norman castle to the north of the village, thus transforming the *Come* of Domesday into the *Castelcumbe* of 1270.

As a wool town, Castle Combe reached the height of its prosperity in the 17th century, and it was during this period that most of its wonderful old houses were constructed. Stone-built weavers' cottages line The Street as it descends to the river, their high pointed gables and steeply pitched roofs designed to clear rainwater quickly from the porous stone tiles.

Villagers would deliver the cloth woven in their cottages to Weavers' House at the bridge, but the heart of the village was the marketplace. There, beside the medieval village pump, stands a fine 14th-century market cross with worn steps and a stone-shingled roof on four columns. Once a market house stood nearby, but this was demolished in the 19th century; an odd pile of stone known locally as the Butter Cross, although perhaps simply a mounting block, marks its position. The Castle Inn Hotel and the White

*OPPOSITE: In 1966 the area around the Pack Bridge was transformed into a fishing-port for the film* Dr Doolittle.

*BELOW: A wealth of exquisitely decorative architectural detail, much of it original, can be found throughout Castle Combe.*

Hart pub complete the scene, while just a little further off is the Old Court House, its jettied half-timbered first floor unusual in this predominantly stone-built village. To the rear of the building the wattle and daub gaol was later used as a garden shed!

The 12th-century church of St Andrews was largely rebuilt in the 19th century, the ancient custom of burying people beneath the walls having undermined the building to a dangerous extent. Nevertheless, the original church tower, erected with the financial assistance of wealthy clothiers, remains intact, complete with its 15th-century faceless clock that once chimed the hours. But the best known structure in the village has to be the 15th-century Pack Bridge over the beautiful By Brook, which is reputedly haunted by a Roman centurion killed during the construction of a much earlier river crossing.

From the reign of Richard II, the village was owned by the Scropes family, only leaving their possession when it was put up for auction in 1947. Lying at the southernmost edge of the Cotswolds, Castle Combe was already a minor tourist attraction by this time, but the attention it was to receive on being named 'Prettiest Village in England' in 1962, proved something of a mixed blessing. The resulting increase in visitors never really subsided. Soon the village was in demand as a film location. Next came the television crews. Yet the funds generated by such interest were ploughed back into the restoration and conservation of the village, enabling it, if anything, to become even prettier. Moreover, the village is now a designated conservation area: its properties listed and most vehicles banished. Hardly surprising then that Castle Combe was voted 'Most Picturesque Village' of 2001.

# BLAISE HAMLET

## AVON

The cottage orné was a key component of the Picturesque style of building and landscape architecture in vogue at the end of the 18th and beginning of the 19th century. It celebrated the asymmetrical and the irregular as essential elements in any effective work of art, thereby defining these qualities as those most gratifying to the eye. Estates were landscaped in such a way that a series of picturesque views were created, into which a sense of animation could be injected by the inclusion of a rustic cottage occupied by folk whose lives were tied to the landscape.

This artificial and exaggerated – yet at the same time idealized – rusticity became highly favoured by wealthy landowners looking to improve the appearance of their

estates. One such was John Scandrett Harford, a Quaker, merchant and banker, who commissioned Humphrey Repton, the leading exponent of Picturesque landscape gardening at the time, to redesign the grounds of his 650-acre Blaise Castle estate. It occupied the site of St Blaise's chapel (St Blasius was the patron Saint of woolcombers and very popular in medieval times) in an area to the north-west of the city of Bristol that had once been a Roman camp. The castle itself was an 18th-century folly and summer house built for the estate's previous owner, Thomas Farr.

Repton created a landscape of drama and romance that included buildings designed in part by the architect John Nash, later friend to the Prince Regent and designer of the Brighton Pavilion. When, in 1809, Harford decided that he would like to add a small group of cottages on Hallen Road for his old retainers (former estate workers who had grown elderly or infirm), Nash produced a stunning collection of nine cottages orné grouped around a green, complete with ornamental trees and a stone pump. No two cottages are alike, yet they are united stylistically by their asymmetry, overstated use of thatch or tile, rustic wooden projections and tall

decorative chimneys. Each set within its own private garden space, the cottages display an astonishing wealth of fine detail: every line, curve and angle has been carefully calculated and measured for optimum impact.

Eccentric in their orientation to the green and to each other, this small group of cottages, known as Blaise Hamlet, is set hard against the estate wall on the outskirts of a major city. It was nevertheless to influence many subsequent estate villages, capturing so perfectly as it did the spirit of romantic nostalgia for an English village that never was.

*ABOVE: Purchased by the Bristol Corporation in 1926, Blaise Hamlet has been in the hands of the National Trust since 1943.*

*OPPOSITE: John Nash designed a stone pump for the green at Blaise Hamlet complete with sundial and weather vane.*

# BIBURY

## GLOUCESTERSHIRE

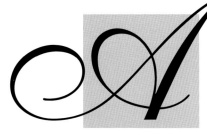

An 8th-century document tells of a woman called Beage who leased an estate called Beaganbyrig, which is Old English for 'stronghold or manor house of a woman called Beage'. Its name had changed to Begeberie by Domesday and it is known today as Bibury. Yet the name most often associated with this rural community is that of the 19th-century artist and poet William Morris, who once described Bibury as 'the most beautiful village in England'.

Water and stone shape Bibury's identity. The long River Colne flows slowly through its heart, spanned by a large road bridge dated 1770, while Bibury Spring disgorges more than nine million litres (two million gallons) of water a day. This abundant source of natural power was exploited to some effect by the 17th-century Arlington Mill, once employed in the fulling of cloth and later used for milling corn, until the machinery was removed to help with the war effort in 1913. Now a museum, there is working machinery here once more, while below the mill lies a thriving trout farm. Founded in 1902, its hatcheries can produce up to ten million rainbow trout each year.

On the opposite side of both river and road stands the Swan, a 17th-century coaching inn, which for some years also played host to the manor court, while close by can be found a tiny octagonal building that served as the village gaol. The other pub in Bibury is the 15th-century Catherine Wheel Inn near the square at the western end of the village. In fact, the Bibury we know today is really made up of two villages: Arlington to the west of the river and Bibury to the east.

The famous terrace of 17th-century stone cottages known as Arlington Row – gabled, stone-tiled and covered in creepers – looks out over narrow floral borders, a pathway and a millstream to the frequently mist-shrouded water meadow of Rack Isle and the river beyond. Rack Isle is so called because it was here that the fulled cloth was laid out on racks to dry. Surrounded by water on three sides and prone to flooding, it has become a protected breeding ground for wildfowl and is owned, like Arlington Row, by the National Trust.

Once a medieval sheephouse or wool store, Arlington Row was converted into weavers' cottages in 1633. The cloth produced within would have been washed in the millstream and then sent on to the nearby Arlington Mill. The buildings are now almshouses and probably the most photographed line of dwellings in the country.

At the eastern end of Bibury, St Mary's Church retains much from its Anglo Saxon beginnings although some objects on display are reproduction (the originals are now in the British Museum). It is tempting to associate these ancient stones with Beage herself, although in all probability they are later. Plenty of Norman and Early English stonework is still in evidence at St Mary's, as well as some delightful 13th-century stained glass while the graveyard is known for its carved Georgian tombstones. Nearby is a fine Jacobean mansion (sometimes attributed to Inigo Jones). Now a hotel it stands on an old site, for there was a Roman villa here once, followed by a Saxon minster and a Norman grange.

Beauty, history and community combine at Bibury; the only thing that spoils the perfect loveliness of this wonderful Cotswold village is the sheer volume of visitors with their cars!

*OPPOSITE: A wonderful Cotswold stone cottage sits in a glorious floral garden. There is little traditional, about this scene however, as cottage gardens were originally used for growing vegetables, with only a small patch for flowers.*

# BISLEY

## GLOUCESTERSHIRE

When the winds blow strong and chill in the valleys around these parts, people have been heard to remark 'Bisley gates are open', for the Cotswold village in question is 240 metres (784 feet) above sea level and clings tenaciously to its exposed position close to the summit of a precipitously steep hill. Subject to the full force of biting gales, the settlement acquired the nickname of 'Bisley-God-Help-Us', and yet, despite the remoteness of its location, there is evidence of human activity in the immediate vicinity from Neolithic times.

Already a thriving community by Domesday, it soon attained pre-eminence in the region, even surpassing nearby Stroud in importance: it was Bisley's name that was attached to the administrative Hundred when it was formed. Its reliable natural springs and location at the intersection of several major routes across the region had encouraged growth but the lines of communication gradually changed and by the mid-18th century nearly all through traffic bypassed Bisley.

Like many other Cotswold villages, Bisley was 'built on wool'. Granted a market by James II, it was then a busy textile community home to large numbers of hand loom weavers, its fine grey-stone houses set into terraces across the face of the hillside (George Street's 17th-century Bear Inn had a particularly imposing facade and was once the court-house). Bisley's main street slopes gently, but steep lanes dive away from it at various angles. Created in the age of the donkey and packhorse, and on difficult terrain, many routes through Bisley remain narrow to this day.

During the prosperous years of the early 18th century, large houses with smooth walls of finely dressed ashlar and steeply gabled stone roofs were built in the lower, more sheltered parts of the expanding town. But Bisley's production methods were fast becoming outmoded and uncompetitive. The resulting decline in fortunes led to later properties being built higher up the hillside in more exposed positions, they were also of

*OPPOSITE: The village of Bisley grew at a crossroads on the wooded northern slopes of the valley of the river Frome.*

humbler construction, with rubble walls and roofs of a lower pitch. Gradually, Bisley's home industries failed and its people started to rely on the mills in the valley for employment, but the end of the war with France in 1815 drastically reduced the need for uniforms and dressings and the textile industry as a whole experienced a significant slump in trade. Things were going from bad to worse for the people of Bisley, so when mechanized production methods reached the mills, it was seen as nothing less than a disaster.

By the 1820s, only one-third of the population, which at that time was around 6,000 people, worked full time in the textile industry, with just a few hundred more as part-time employees. The first year of Queen Victoria's reign (1837) was a time of great poverty in Bisley, so much so that on 31 August of that year 68 people emigrated to the New World, their expenses being paid by public subscription. Bisley even acquired a new nickname of 'Beggarly Bisley', and when people identified their home as 'Bisley-God-Help-Us' the old nickname took on a whole new meaning.

The loss of its market made Bisley a village once more, its fine buildings falling into disuse and decay including the parish church of All Saints, built over the course of the 13th and 14th centuries. When the new rector, 33-year-old Thomas Keble, arrived in 1827, he found the roof of the nave being propped up by a fir tree and no glass in the windows, so that people were using them as doorways. In the decades that followed, he set about raising sufficient funds to have the church restored.

Keble also renovated the five water chutes known as the Bisley Wells that originated from springs beneath the churchyard and which provided the main

fresh water supply for the village. When the well head was replaced in 1863, two further chutes were added. Keble then borrowed a tradition from Derbyshire when he inaugurated an annual well-dressing ceremony.

Thomas Keble remained rector of Bisley for nearly 50 years. He had taken the village in hand, reviving both the spirit and the fabric of the place, and to him must be due much of the credit for the fact that today this very smart and attractive village is far from 'Beggarly'

*ABOVE: Bisley's steeply sloping lanes are lined with handsome stone cottages and houses constructed mainly in the 18th century.*

# SNOWSHILL
## GLOUCESTERSHIRE

There has been a small upland settlement at Snowshill for many centuries, clinging to the wooded slopes high on the Cotswold escarpment, yet the metalled road to the nearby village of Broadway was completed only in 1872. Before that, a network of ancient trackways was the only means of communication. Bearing in mind that the village's name is derived from the Old English Snaw-hyll, meaning 'hill where the snow lies long', its tight-knit community needed to be determinedly self-sufficient, especially through the long winter months of isolation.

The exposed hillside pastures of Snowshill with their spectacular views over the valley below were once part of the vast sheep estates owned by Winchcombe Abbey. Cotswold wool was famous throughout Europe in the 14th century, but there is no magnificent 'wool' church at Snowshill to show for it. Rebuilt in 1864, the stone edifice of St Barnabus stands on the village's small sloping green hunched beneath its oddly truncated tower (lack of funds preventing construction of the intended spire).

Snowshill Manor is the real treasure of the village. Originally a Tudor hall house it once belonged to Henry VIII's wife Catherine Parr, but has been much converted over

*RIGHT: Unspoilt cottages built of warm Cotswold limestone surround the 19<sup>th</sup> century church of St Barnabus. Snowshill is one of the most beautifully situated villages on the Cotswold Way long distance footpath.*

*Right: This charming, yet almost hidden village has featured in several television and film productions, the most recent being Bridget Jones's Diary.*

over the centuries and now resembles a small Georgian mansion. For many years it was simply a farmhouse. Then in 1919, neglected and near-derelict, it was purchased by Charles Paget Wade, who had it carefully restored using traditional methods and materials, to house his outstanding collection of curious and rare objects from all over the globe. It is said that J. M. Barrie found the inspiration for Peter Pan while a guest at Snowshill Manor though Charles Wade himself never lived there preferring a converted cottage on the estate known as Priest's House, a reminder of the days when the manor was monastic land. In 1951, he gave the house, its contents and gardens to the National Trust for all to enjoy.

The village of Snowshill may lack the romantic perfection of its near neighbour, Stanton (where Barrie is supposed to have dreamed up Tinkerbell) but it is replete with genuine character and interest. An alehouse for much of its seven centuries, the Snowshill Arms with its traditional skittle alley remains popular today with locals and visitors alike, while around the green range superb buildings in warm, golden limestone, plus delightful old stone cottages with little gabled dormers under roofs of local slate.

Although sheep still roam the surrounding hillsides, many of Snowshill's residents are retired, the main employers in the village being the National Trust and the pub. Snowshill lavender has become famous, but many who visit the lavender fields never venture into the village itself. Self-sufficient no more, its single shop closed when the lady who owned it retired, so now shopping is done in Broadway or Evesham, while the children take the coach to school in Chipping Camden.

# ALLERFORD & SELWORTHY

## SOMERSET

llerford and Selworthy are adjacent villages linked since Domesday, yet today they are very different from one another in character. In 1086, Ralph de Limesey held the manors of Allerford and Selworthy, among others, but by the 18th century they were in the hands of the Aclands, who at one point owned estates that stretched from Minehead to Exeter. Since 1944, the 12,500 acres of the Holnicote estate, including the villages of Allerford and Selworthy, have been in the possession of the National Trust.

Always the larger and more village-like of the two settlements, Allerford is divided into Higher Allerford – a small group of buildings on the hillside including a 15th-century longhouse and several cottages – and Lower Allerford on the eastern side of the River Aller. The village straggles along the lane that joins the two, its attractive cottages and farmhouses, made of local red rubble stone and often colourwashed, dating from the late 18th to early 19th centuries, with the occasional 20th-century newcomer. Selworthy Village School, a thatched early 19th-century building, and actually situated in Allerford, has become a fascinating museum of rural life while children from the villages now travel to Minehead for their education. Almost opposite the school is the

combined post office and village stores, a short distance from Selworthy Parish Hall, also in Allerford!

Meanwhile, at Selworthy itself, Sir Thomas Acland's mid-19th-century philanthropic remodelling of the medieval farmhouses that dotted the formerly treeless slopes was described as a 'perfect village' by Beatrix Potter. Little can be seen from the leafy lane that ascends the steep hill to the splendid church for the many trees planted as part of Sir Thomas's original design have grown tall and broad, hiding the dwellings from sight. Unfortunately, the concrete render covering the church continually shrugs off its coating of lime wash and tallow, leaving it rather sorry-looking at times, but magnificent when freshly painted. A small gate opposite the great stone tithe barn (situated on glebe land to the east) gives access to a narrow winding pathway. This leads to a long village green, around which stand cream-washed thatched cottages with delightful dormer windows and tall chimneys surrounded by neat garden plots. Built in the Picturesque style fashionable at the time and possibly influenced by John Harford's Blaise Hamlet (see page 68-9), they were constructed to accommodate the old retainers of the Holnicote Estate, who would have walked the level paths to Allerford for their provisions, sporting fine red cloaks denoting their special status.

Selworthy has, like its former inhabitants, settled into comfortable retirement, becoming an inhabited tourist attraction while neighbouring Allerford, although no longer on the busy A39 following some road straightening, must continue to agonize over rural issues such as local unemployment and the shortage of affordable housing.

# DUNSTER

## SOMERSET

Though its origins are far older, Dunster's story really begins shortly after the Norman Conquest when William the Conqueror gave William de Mohun no fewer than 69 manors in this part of England. Work on Dunster Castle commenced almost immediately, for it was to be de Mohun's administrative centre. Standing in Dunster's enclosed main street, you would never guess that you are only 3km (2 miles) from the sea. It is equally hard to believe that before the mouth of its river silted up, the settlement was a trading port for local produce and Welsh wool, with a busy harbour boasting several shipbuilding and repair yards as well as a small fishing industry.

More widely known is that Dunster became both wealthy and famous through the manufacture of a type of heavy cloth that came to bear its name. For a time nearly every villager would have been involved in the cottage industries of spinning and

weaving. There were also several fulling mills where the cloth was washed and thickened, and the imposing Yarn Market is as instantly recognizable as the castle, perhaps even more so. Standing implacably in the middle of High Street, it has presided over trade and commerce here since 1580, but there have been markets and fairs in Dunster since the 13th century.

There are in fact two sides to Dunster, and they are quite different. High Street is the commercial heart of the old medieval town: a wide street lined with thriving shops and businesses as well as impressive medieval buildings such as the 15th-century Luttrell Arms, once the house of the Abbot of Cleeve. It became an inn during the 17th century and was named after the family who owned the castle for 600 years. There is also a 15th-century slate-hung nunnery in Church Street, which has rarely seen a nun, having been used primarily as a guest house for the priory.

The transition at Dunster occurs behind the church, among the remains of the 11th-century priory, which includes a large Norman dovecote, 14th-century priest's house, 16th-century tithe barn and walled cloister garden complete with herbs. For as you travel further along West Street and into Mill Lane, you find the medieval urban landscape has vanished. You are now in the open countryside where the footpaths have names such as 'Ducky' and 'Goosey'. The Domesday survey found two mills here; the one which can be seen today dates from the 17th century, but may stand on the site of one of the original buildings. Here, there are cob and thatch cottages in pretty gardens and an ancient packhorse bridge over the River Avill. The latter was once called Doddebridge, but has been known as Gallox Bridge ever since gallows were placed at the nearby crossroads.

Visitors flock to Dunster all year round. The commanding red-sandstone castle is now in the hands of the National Trust, while the working mill and associated tea rooms are open from spring to autumn. But one of the most magical events of the year takes place just before Christmas. For two evenings, all the buildings along the three main streets are lit by candlelight. A procession takes place, in which stilt walkers in colourful costumes put up lanterns, accompanied by a host of traditional street performers while at the watermill, the miller works by candlelight.

Dunster was in the thick of the English Civil Wars, and has seen its castle besieged and then fall. It lost its harbour but survived; it lost its wool trade, too, and survived that also; and its railway station opened in 1874 only to close again just short of its centenary. Yet today Dunster is as busy as ever, having discovered that its niche in the tourist market is almost as lucrative as its former enterprises.

*LEFT: 'Dunster Medieval Village.' As High Street sweeps away into Church Street and with the Norman castle rising before you, it almost seems possible to hear the sounds of a medieval marketplace.*

# The Eastern Counties

Bedfordshire's high Chiltern Hills give way to the flat lands and wide open skies of East Anglia, while to the north the rolling Lincolnshire Wolds are reminiscent of the varied undulations of Hertfordshire. This is a gentle landscape, although the icy winds that sometimes blast across the low areas of reclaimed coastal marsh and fenland, while an excellent source of natural power, can often make you feel that you are much further north.

Now one of the most sparsely inhabited regions in the country, East Anglia was once the most densely populated. The Breckland was home to England's oldest industry – flint knapping (the shaping of flint to make tools, weapons or building stone) – while Suffolk spent several centuries at the heart of the nation's single most important – woollen manufacture. But East Anglia's lack of an extensive communications network – it had only a few good roads – and its shortage of local raw materials meant that the region got rather left behind as the Industrial Revolution gathered pace. Instead, it fell back on agriculture, which had been progressing steadily in the background all along. However, the counties on the margins of eastern England, being closer to the metropolis or to the Midlands, prospered, and as a consequence, were far more susceptible to change.

LEFT: A delightful timber-framed cottage in Hemingford Grey. The eastern counties have enjoyed mixed fortunes in terms of the survivability of their old architecture due to the lack of local building stone. Walls of chalk clunch or mud and straw perished quickly while masterpieces of timber construction or brick endure.

# FINCHINGFIELD

## ESSEX

*F*inchingfield is a village that leaves a lasting impression on all who visit: its appeal, though enigmatic, is nevertheless very real. A large triangular green – one of two in the village – is divided into oddly shaped pieces by roads and leads to a broad stream-fed pond crossed by a small brick bridge. At one side stands the Fox, a beautifully pargeted 18th-century coaching inn situated in a prime position at the intersection of several routes. Ahead an attractive jumble of houses and cottages climbs the hill to the 15th-century guildhall with the church of St John the Baptist rising behind.

Prior to a storm of uncertain date, but in the region of 300 years ago, a spire graced the 12th-century tower. How different the famous view would look had it not been toppled, for the 18th-century cupola, which now contains the medieval angelus bell, is one of Finchingfield's most distinctive features. Thankfully, the wonderful old timber-framed guildhall, built virtually within the churchyard, was not damaged. It had another lucky escape in 1905 when the adjacent building, then the Green Man pub, burned to the ground. Only the quick response of the local horsedrawn fire engine, assisted by another from Wethersfield, managed to prevent the flames spread-

OPPOSITE: *Finchingfield is a former spinning village whose green, pond, cottages and church combine to create a 'typical' English village scene.*

BELOW: *In a village where no two buildings are exactly alike the unplanned nature of their arrangement only serves to enhance the overall effect.*

ing but the pub, ironically also the local office of the Sun Insurance Company, could not be saved. Presumably there was no problem with the insurance payout because the Green Man was soon rebuilt! Later renamed the Finch, the property has recently been converted from a public to a private house, leaving just the Fox, Red Lion and Three Tuns to serve the 1,200-plus residents and their many summer visitors.

Fine weather always draws crowds of sightseers to Finchingfield. Picnickers do battle with ducks and geese for a spot on the green, while many come to admire the gleaming white post mill at Duck End, to the north of the village. There were once several windmills in the parish, but this is the only one that survives, and it is said that there has been a windmill on this site since 1100. Dating from 1756, the present example was last used commercially at the end of the 19th century before falling into disrepair. Now beautifully restored, it is one of the most picturesque elements of this part of the village. This is also where Finchingfield's fine collection of thatched cottages can be found, including a hexagonal one that is known by locals as the Pepperpot.

Manufacturers of jigsaws and picture calendars have long recognized the appeal of this lovely village whose image has become famous world-wide.

# WENDENS AMBO

## ESSEX

*I*n 1086, the Domesday Book recorded two villages here: Wenden Magna, which at slightly more than 800 acres sustained a population of just under 100 souls; and Wenden Parva, one-quarter the size of its neighbour but with nearly half the population. Wendens Ambo was not to become a single parish until 1662, 'ambo' being Latin for 'both', while the name 'Wendens' is derived from the Old English word for winding, a reference to the tortuous meanderings of a stream through the villages.

By the 17th century, the village consisted of several large farms and their associated outbuildings, plus some smaller holdings in between once the two villages were joined. However, livestock farming suffered a downturn in the next 100 years, and although the village switched emphasis from animals to wheat its fortunes did not recover until the railway arrived in 1845. The station is still an important link with the capital and other large towns in the vicinity, for the majority of villagers are of working age and those not employed at the nearby business park commute daily.

*OPPOSITE: Church Path cottages. In the churchyard nearby lies Midshipman Nicholson, who was served under Nelson on the Vanguard.*

*BELOW: Brightly colour-washed and tiled, or whitewashed and heavily thatched, many cottages in the village are surrounded by colourful gardens.*

Wendens Ambo has developed around a tight double bend in the B1039 that also descends a steep hill. The much-used village hall sits high above the diminutive church of St Mary the Virgin, which nestles in a cluster of trees amid rolling farmland. The best approach to the church is from halfway down the hill, along a pretty cul-de-sac called Church Path. Here is one of Wendens Ambo's best-loved scenes: a picturesque row of cottages on a high grass bank that ascends to the ancient place of worship. This close to the county border, you can forgive St Mary's its Hertfordshire 'spike' spire, especially when you see the early Norman tower doorway with its recycled Roman bricks and discover the wonderful 15th-century frescoes within.

From the churchyard can be glimpsed the outbuildings of Wenden Hall, an impressive farmhouse dating, in part, to the 15th century but which is somewhat overshadowed by its magnificent timber-framed, tri-gabled thatched barn. The hall's driveway leads out into the appropriately named Duck Street, the ground being damp and marshy, while opposite a house called Trout Hall there is a large tree-lined pool. Nearby is a 16th-century inn, the Bell; its bowed timber-framed walls and partly jettied first floor plastered and painted dark red. In the curving tiled roof stands an enormous chimney, the old building around it appearing to buckle and stoop over the busy road with no pavement to act as a buffer.

In 1972, residents concerned by the proximity of the M11 and a proposed housing development, set up the Wendens Ambo Society to promote and preserve the rich but fragile heritage of the village and actively participate in shaping its future.

# ALDBURY

## HERTFORDSHIRE

With the dire state of rural public transport being such an important issue for many villagers, it might be impolitic to suggest that the car park in a living village such as Aldbury 'spoils the view'. Lauded as the loveliest of all Hertfordshire villages, Aldbury, although extremely well kept, has ever been carefree about its looks. While clearly proud of its many picturesque and aged treasures, this is a working community that welcomes visitors without actively courting them.

Yet were it not for the car park, situated inconveniently for photographers right in the middle of what is probably the most visually interesting part of the village, it would be difficult to find fault with the place. A triangular green covers the heart of the village, within which sits a large duck pond, like a vast muddy puddle. To one side stand a young oak and some old stocks. It is a scene reflected many times over in the shimmering lattice windows of the Old Manor House, a name assumed rather than descriptive since the property has only ever been the home of yeomen farmers. Now comprising two comfortable dwellings, it once held four, as well as the village reading room, within its walls of mellow bricks and darkened timbers. In close proximity are a creeper-clad, 200-year-old pub (standing on the site of a much older hostelry), the combined village store and post office, and the tiny, tall-chimneyed village bakehouse, while behind them rises the noble, flint-faced tower of the 13th-century church. It is a scene much loved by artists, for they at least can leave the cars out of their paintings!

When the Saxons first discovered this site, in a dry valley sheltering beneath a high ridge of the Chiltern escarpment, they also saw something about which we can only speculate. For they named their settlement Ald-beri, or 'old fort', though no trace of a stronghold has yet been found here. The Romans seem only to have built a road through the area, but perhaps the Saxons misunderstood the

*OPPOSITE: With its many attractive houses Aldbury's place in the list of Hertfordshire's most popular beauty spots is well deserved.*

purpose of the vast boundary dykes to the north-west that were dug out in the Iron Age. Suffice to say that the Normans found a well established settlement of a dozen or more families when they surveyed in 1086.

This small community of tenant farmers prospered, along with the attendant blacksmiths and other necessary craftsmen. By the late 17th century, many of Aldbury's finest houses were already standing. Sheep grazed the hills, while in the valley a system of open field farming was in operation. One hundred years later, cattle had become the stock animal of choice and many smallholders had been bought out by the larger farming families, who went on to consolidate their holdings, while some of the wealthier tradesmen were building numbers of new cottages for rent. A cottage industry in straw plaiting developed as the downturn in agricultural fortunes took effect during the second half of the 19th century. A generation later the old, dilapidated properties were being taken on and renovated by incomers, attracted by both the scenic location and the excellent rail links with the capital.

With no squire in residence since the mid-17th century, the role of village 'elite' had been filled by the rector and the Duncombe family, who lived in a large farmhouse called Stocks. Eventually the Duncombes removed to the Georgian mansion they had built nearby, taking the name of the house with them. Stocks would later become the home of the Victorian novelist, Mrs Humphrey Ward, who featured much of the village in her work.

Horses rather than cattle roam the pastures these days and the old shops and workshops, half-timbered farmhouses, plait schools and alehouses are now, to the casual observer at least, indistinguishable from each other in their new roles as private dwellings. Water carts are not backed into the pond to fill up as they once were, nor are the lanes around its margin dusty and rough-edged, but on May Day the celebrations on the green are eloquent proof (if any were needed) that the old traditions can live just as happily in an updated setting.

*ABOVE: Aldbury's pond is fed by rain and run-off from the nearby hills. The restored Victorian stocks and whipping post stand at its edge.*

# WESTMILL

## HERTFORDSHIRE

There is no longer any sign of the 'Westerly Mill' that gave this settlement its name, although there were three mills in the village on the banks of the River Ribb at the time of the Domesday survey. With no other for many miles, the millers of Westmill provided a vital service for a wide area.

St Mary's church, Westmill, has Saxon origins and would have been standing, in some form, when the Domesday commissioners called. Much added to and altered in the 14th and 15th centuries, its three bells were sold in the early 19th century to finance urgent structural repairs. A more thorough restoration of 1876, while preserving the physical integrity of the structure, sadly also destroyed much of its former charm.

It is said that a highwayman is buried in the churchyard. Shot dead by his intended victim, he was interred there in an unmarked grave. The following day a grand coach arrived in the village. Its mysterious female occupant ordered that the body be exhumed. She was obeyed, and upon seeing the dead man's face she simply nodded once, as if in recognition, then climbed back into her coach and drove away. While the veracity of this story can only be guessed at, it is known that in 1798 the death of a Westmill man, John Mellish MP, was England's last recorded murder by a highwayman.

Not far away, the pink-washed Sword in Hand pub is thought to be the oldest inhabited structure in the village, having been built more than 500 years ago. Once the manor house of the Bellendens in the 18th century, it was known as the Old House even then. At the beginning of the 19th century, it became an inn, its name inspired by the family crest of the Gregs, who were the squires at that time. Recently the present owners were intrigued to discover a mummified cat hidden in the loft space. In folklore such animals were said to ward off evil spirits and bring good luck, but, unfortunately, the one at Westmill was so decayed it all but disintegrated when handled. Not long afterwards, fire swept through the upper part of the building, which later caused the landlady to ponder whether it might have been better to have left the cat where it was! Thankfully, nobody was injured and the historic old structure remained sufficiently intact to be repaired and subsequently enjoyed by the many visitors who crowd its ancient high-ceilinged rooms in the summer months. A charming thatched black-and-white timber-framed building stands to one side of the main street, while along the Aspenden road, the partly thatched Dial Cottage, with its beautiful cottage garden, is unashamedly from three periods, boasting three different roof heights and two types of roofing material.

Westmill can boast several more fine old buildings; the 15th century Archers Hall being a particularly good example, with its tiny casements and pargeted front. Even so, the village's best known feature is its triangular green. Bordered on three sides by cottages, a quaint village hall and an attractive combined tea rooms, post office and shop line the fourth. An ornate pump stands near the centre of the green beneath a decorative lantern, hanging from an elegant tiled canopy on five timber posts. Its heavily carved wooden cap is engraved with a line from the 19th-century South African poet Elisa Cook: 'Traverse the Desert and Then Ye Can Tell What Treasure Exists in The Cool Deep Well'. But the real treasure in Westmill is its people who every summer hold an immensely popular village fête to raise funds for local charities and community groups.

With the village working together for a common cause in a spirit of mutual support and cooperation, it is reminiscent of the days when such sentiments were everyday necessities of village life.

# TURVEY

## BEDFORDSHIRE

*I*t takes an old bridge of sixteen grey stone arches plus a causeway to ford the River Ouse at Turvey; part of the way across, Buckinghamshire meets Bedfordshire. Although the earliest recorded bridge at this location was built in around 1140, the region's gently undulating, fertile land had already enticed the ancient Beaker People to settle in the vicinity. More recently, the Romans were here.

The 13th century must have been a prosperous time for Turvey because as well as laying the foundations for the present bridge, the locals were making their mark on the parish church. Saxon in origin, All Saints was first built here in AD 980, although the present structure is largely medieval. Its treasures include a

*RIGHT: Eccentrically patterned brickwork decorates the end wall of the rectory, which was rebuilt in 1839. One former occupant, the Reverend G F W Munby wrote several books about the village and its history.*

magnificently decorative 13th-century oak door and a 14th-century fresco of the crucifixion.

Present-day Turvey owes much of its appearance and appeal to the Higgins family. As lords of the manor, they were responsible for rebuilding much of the village during the course of the 19th century. Nevertheless many of Turvey's old buildings remain. The village store was once the Tinker of Turvey Inn, where a well known tinker lived with his wife and dog. Rumoured to have its origins in the mid-12th century, the inn used to boast a sign that read: 'The Tinker of Turvey, his dog and his staff, Old Nell and her budget would make a man laugh', a budget being a traveller's pack. Nell, it seems, was just as famous as her husband, for Nell's Well produced fresh drinking water from its

archway near Ladybridge Terrace from 1600 until 1960, when it was closed by the authorities amid much public outcry.

Also of great age is the Three Fyshes inn, which dates from 1622 and has survived more than one severe flood if the levels marked on its wall are anything to go by. Some old farmworker's cottages also survive, originally built for labourers on the Turvey Abbey estate in the 17th century. The abbey itself was in reality a substantial Jacobean manor house, only becoming a religious house when purchased by Benedictine monks in the 1980s.

At one time the village could boast two flourishing cottage industries typical of the area. Lacemaking had been introduced to the region in the late 16th century, probably by Huguenot refugees. Soon specialist lace schools had been set up in local cottages. Whole families might be employed in this way, with even small children working their bobbins from dawn till dusk to patterns handed down through the generations. Straw plaiting, on the other hand, was easier but less remunerative. The raw material, brought to Bedfordshire from East Anglia and the Chilterns, was split into thin, workable strips, and the finished product sewn together to make hats. However, the traditional trades that once made Turvey all but self-sufficient have died out one by one. The smithy has gone and the old bakehouse is now a private residence. The old school is now the village hall and a field where agricultural experiments took place in the 19th century has now become the green.

In the 1870s, the arrival of the railway brought rapid change. With five trains a day, the population of Turvey at once became mobile and began to grow. Today, there are 20th-century housing estates to cope with the rise in population, while the problem caused by cars using the main road, which passes through the village, has led villagers to campaign for a bypass.

# STEVINGTON

## BEDFORDSHIRE

*'He came at a place somewhat ascending; and upon that place stood a cross, and a little below, in the bottom a sepulchre'.* Pilgrim's Progress, John Bunyan, 1678

The cross where Bunyan's Christian shook off his burden was a 14th-century market cross of possibly Celtic origin and the sepulchre into which it tumbled had once been a pagan shrine, but by Bunyan's day they had acquired an altered significance. It was upon the steps of Stevington's cross that John Bunyan stood and preached to the local people, thus founding a Baptist meeting in the village, while a short distance down the hill the water that flowed from a rock below St Mary's churchyard wall had become a holy well that attracted many pilgrims.

Today, visitors to Stevington are likely to be ramblers stopping off at the Royal George or the Red Lion to pick up the key to the village's wonderfully restored working mill, for Stevington is set on a terrace above the Great Ouse, which is in its meandering youth here. Church Lane leads the walker out from shady streets lined with mellow stone cottages into beautiful water meadows and a landscape divided and neatly packaged by early 19th-century enclosures.

Life here has not always been so tranquil. Lying between Watling Street and Ermine Street, this 'farmstead belonging to a man called Stiffa' may well have been bypassed by the Romans, but the Danish invasions of the 9th century AD saw the settlement turned into a frontier village. Until its recapture in AD 915, Bedford – which is only 11km (7 miles) distant – fell within the area of Danelaw. When more peaceful times returned, Stevington thrived and seemingly as a demonstration of optimism and determination, the solidly square Saxon tower of St Mary's was raised. By Domesday, the former Mercian village of Stiuentone was one of the wealthiest in the region for its size.

Fragments of today's village date from the 16th century, and the church contains a fine brass memorial to Sir Thomas de Salle, a 15th-century knight. But most of what we see is from the 17th century or later. Some parts may well have been familiar to Bunyan, although the village's handsome Baptist church was not built until 30 years after his death. Over the centuries, the paths between the dwellings and the lanes out to the fields have undergone subtle changes in position and importance, while the 19th century saw the introduction of brick-built cottages fashioned from materials supplied by a local brickfield.

Nevertheless, Stevington remains centred on its crossroads with its large and decorative cross, while the four arms that radiate from this enclosed point wind away in a jumble of steep thatch and low slate or pantile roofs above houses of many sizes and surfaces. Around every bend, natural stone mixes with colour-washed brick or plaster. Some cottages open directly onto the road, while others shelter behind narrow green verges or small walled gardens. Once the dwellings of farmers and labourers, traditional Bedfordshire lacemakers and the mat makers who gathered rushes from the riverbanks, they are now the well-kept homes of a mature population, largely retired, which relishes the rare tranquillity of Stevington's beautiful rural setting.

The ancient almshouses remain, but the old manor house and great medieval tithe barn were demolished in the late 19th century. They once stood opposite the old schoolhouse, which is a well preserved survivor. Built in 1863, the British School opened the following year but in the second half of the 20th century the number of pupils steadily dwindled until in 1983 the school closed its doors to students for the last time.

With no school and no shop, much of the activity in the village is to be found around the three churches – Church of England, Baptist and Methodist – and the two public houses: the old Royal George in Silver Street, a former 17th-century coaching inn re-named by a former sailor-turned-landlord after the flagship of Admiral Kempenfelt which sank off Spithead in 1782, and the younger and bolder Red Lion, which stands on one corner of the crossroads. It is here that you may seek the key to the 18th-century post mill which, although it has ground no corn since 1936, remains one of the most important features in the local landscape.

OPPOSITE:
Stevington's Silver Street is lined with dwellings of all shapes, sizes and materials. The building on the far right of the picture is the Royal George.

LEFT: Stevington's 14th century market cross stands in the middle of the crossroads with the red brick Red Lion behind occupying the corner of Park Road.

The Rupert Brooke

# GRANTCHESTER
## CAMBRIDGESHIRE

Grantchester is a quiet village on the outskirts of Cambridge. Celebrated in the verse of Rupert Brooke, the village as he described it now represents, for many people, the essence of the English village. As a fluid Saxon settlement, Grantchester reoriented itself as needs directed but there may have been a Roman camp here long before that time, while numerous Bronze Age artefacts suggest even earlier habitation.

Much added to, rebuilt and extended, the parish church of St Andrew and St Mary has its origins in early Norman times, while much of the village has been, at one time or another, in the hands of the great universities of Oxford and Cambridge. Grantchester mill (with adjacent land) formed part of the original endowment of Merton College, Oxford, in the 13th century. Later, King's College, Cambridge,

became lord of the manor of Grantchester when it purchased the manor house in 1452. The manor farm became a 'home farm' for the college, providing pigeons from the 'great duff-house', as well as vegetables and medicinal herbs, not to mention an occasional place of refuge from the plague. Meanwhile, Merton College, Oxford collected part of its rent from the mill in the form of eels from the millstream.

Grantchester's romantic pastoral tranquillity is a relatively recent development. Prior to enclosure at the beginning of the 19th century, the village's restful meadows had been made up of labour-intensive strips spread across vast open fields, while a relaxing punt on the river would have been all but impossible due to the barges plying to and from the complex of buildings that made up the enormous mill at the bridge (burned down in 1928). Yet it is for poets and their fascinating circle of friends that the village became known.

Byron's Pool is the spot where, as an undergraduate at Trinity College, Cambridge, the young poet would often dive and swim. Once known as Old Mills, the pool was probably the remnants of a millpond that belonged to one of Grantchester's two Domesday mills.

Probably better known is the attractive Old Vicarage, a mellow brick house from the mid-17th century that will forever be associated with Rupert Brooke. In the late 1860s, its then owner, Samuel Page Widnall, planted an orchard of apple, pear, plum and quince trees there. Thirty years later, the lady who would one day rent rooms in the adjacent Orchard House to Brooke began the tradition of tea in the orchard with the customary homemade scones dripping in honey from the beehives of the Old Vicarage.

Grantchester today is a pleasant accumulation of old thatched cottages, together with more recent brick structures topped with a variety of slates and tiles. The tiny one-room school, later the reading room, is now attached to the village hall, and several of the old pubs remain. New housing in the form of an estate located to the north drew another 200 people into the village in the 1960s, although few of today's 600 or so villagers work in Grantchester itself.

Unsurprisingly, the Orchard Tea Rooms are as popular as ever, and people still flock to Grantchester in search of Brooke's village. Of course, 'his' Grantchester was as much a creation of time as of place. Even though the fabric of the village remains much as he would have known it, its identity and spirit have been altered by the times in which we live, and thus it affords only a glimpse of the place he knew and loved.

*ABOVE: Long used for transportation, communication and now leisure, the beautiful River Cam (or Granta) also powered a large mill, of which only a fragment now remains.*

*OPPOSITE: Grantchester boasts many picturesque cottages of diverse styles and methods of construction.*

# THE HEMINGFORDS
## CAMBRIDGESHIRE

Connected by a short lane, the neigbouring villages of Hemingford Grey and Hemingford Abbots were once part of the same estate, known in Saxon times as Hemmingeford, meaning the 'ford of the people of a man called Hemma'. Danish invaders divided the estate in the 9th century AD and created a new settlement to the east at Thorpe, its name denoting its status as a secondary settlement. A century later, Ailwin, Earl of East Anglia, gave the Hemingford manors to the newly founded Ramsey Abbey. Thus, the larger of the two became known as Hemingford Abbots and the smaller as Hemingford Parva (it would not be given its present name until the de Grey family purchased the estate in 1276). Today, the roles have been reversed and Hemingford Grey is far larger than its neighbour.

Close as they are and with both bordered to the north by the banks of the River Ouse, the villages nonetheless have quite different sites. The southern part of Hemingford Abbots stands high and dry, 33m (100 feet) above sea level, although the land nearer the river is prone to flooding. Hemingford Grey, on the other hand, is entirely low-lying, being only 6–12m (20–40 feet) or so above sea level. In addition, the main street of Hemingford Abbots follows the course of the river, while most of Hemingford Grey's early development took place along two streets, which lead off from the river at right angles.

In both Hemingfords, the manor house, church and rectory can be found close to the river; in the case of Hemingford Grey, they are on the riverbank itself. Here, in the

*RIGHT: The 'Music Room' in the Manor House at Hemingford Grey. The deep window recess shows the thickness of the Norman walls.*

mid-12th century, a tenant of Ramsey Abbey known as Payn of Hemingford started work on a magnificent two-storey moated house made of stone from Northamptonshire. Though much altered and extended over the years, the Manor House retains many original features including the Norman windows and fireplace

Readers of the *Green Knowe* children's books written by Lucy Boston will already be aware that the land surrounding the manor house regularly floods. Thought to be one of the oldest inhabited structures in England, the house was purchased by the author in 1939 and would feature prominently in her work. During the Second World War, Boston wanted to do something for the airmen stationed at nearby RAF Wyton, and so she held musical evenings in the old hall during which the young men would crowd around the large horn of a gramophone.

Payn of Hemingford might also have been responsible for the beginnings of St James's Church in the village. With its unusual truncated tower, the top of which is said to lie at the bottom of the river following a storm in 1741, it creates a picturesque riverside scene. No church was assessed here for the Domesday Book, but in Hemingford Abbots there had been a wooden church since at least AD 974. A stone replacement was built in 1190 which gained a spire in the 13th century, wall paintings in the 15th century, and a century later still, a higher roof with 22 angels.

Both villages contain wonderful examples of old timber-framed thatched cottages from the 16th century onwards, many of them attractively colour-washed. The thatched Axe and Compass pub in Hemingford Abbots dates from the 17th century. Inside, there are many old photographs on display illustrating the history of the community and, as there is no shop in the village, the pub has been known to sell stamps, confectionery and the like. Hemingford Grey, now extensively built-up on its outskirts, has both a pub (the Cock Inn and Restaurant) and a village shop. It also has a post office and

a thriving school. Many of its villagers work from home, whereas Hemingford Abbots is largely a dormitory village. However, both settlements remain surrounded by arable fields and beautiful water meadows.

Hemingford Grey's water mills have long gone, although a windmill remains, while the only trace of the village green is a widening of the road. The village's heyday was when horse-drawn coal barges on the River Ouse made it their habitual stopping place. Now the riverside is the venue for a training and conference centre at the 17th-century Hemingford House. Over at Hemingford Abbots, the highlight of the year is the flower festival during which the church is decorated with stunning floral arrangements and many of the villagers open their delightful gardens to the public.

*ABOVE: Hemingford Abbots has many wonderful thatched properties and the villagers, gardens are a delight with 30 of them being opened to the public during the annual flower festival.*

# HOUGHTON & WYTON

## CAMBRIDGESHIRE

*I*n Saxon times, Houghton and Wyton were distinct settlements, but centuries of gradual expansion has joined them and now they are always referred to in conjunction. Lying between the River Ouse to the south and the Huntingdon to St Ives road in the north, Houghton's fame rests on its magnificent 17th-century wooden water mill, while Wyton gave its name to a 20th-century RAF base.

Linked with Wyton for centuries, by both proximity and ownership, Houghton is undoubtedly the dominant partner today, but when assessed by the Domesday commissioners in 1086 the two were of roughly similar size. In the 10th century, possession of the two villages and the mill at Houghton passed from Ailwin, Earl of East Anglia, to the abbey he had founded at Ramsey, 16km (10 miles) distant. Later, the parishes of Houghton and Wyton would be enclosed together under a single act of 1773, but they did not officially become united as one civil parish until 1935.

Now in the hands of the National Trust, the four-storey mill at Houghton is the last in a long line of such structures erected on or near to this site. Standing on a man-made island, it once had a wheel on three sides, each driving a pair of stones. In medieval

*OPPOSITE: Now divided into two private dwellings, the former George & Dragon once had a central hall open to the rafters.*

times, all tenants of the abbey faced a hefty fine if they took their corn elsewhere and disputes between villagers and the mill's owners were common.

On the abbey's dissolution in 1539, the manor of Houghton-cum-Wyton became crown property, and so it remained for more than a century until sold by Charles I in 1625. In the 19th century, the mill, together with a farm, was leased by Quaker merchant, Potto Brown, and his partner, Joseph Goodman for the sum of £352 a year, which in 1852 was a considerable amount of money. Brown was a philanthropist as well as a shrewd businessman. Although he had received little formal education himself he set up a school for the villages. In 1840, together with Goodman, he was responsible for the construction of the yellow-brick Union Chapel in Houghton. He also donated the village pump on Houghton's green. Gothic in style, this cast-iron pump is unique in the county and has a Grade II listing. On Brown's death in 1871, his son Bateman took over the mill and a bronze bust of the great man was commissioned in recognition of all he had done for the villages. Houghton's unusual thatched clock tower and shelter was erected in 1902 in remembrance of another of Potto's sons, George William Brown.

Houghton's oldest house, built towards the end of the 15th century, was the home of a yeoman farmer before becoming the George & Dragon inn for a time. Today, the Three Horseshoes on the eastern side of the green is Houghton's only public house, while Wyton has the Three Jolly Butchers. Built in 1622, this is another converted yeoman's dwelling and once sported a fine thatched roof, although now it is

tiled. Another successful conversion can be found near the clock tower in Houghton, where two out of a terrace of five 17th-century cottages have become Ye Olde Village Shoppe. Serving as a general store and post office, it has three bay windows that are a picture when dressed at Christmas time.

Houghton and Wyton are doubly blessed with a fine old church each. However, their real delight is the riverbank. Here, the Ouse splits into a series of channels that flow slowly through delightful water meadows, popular with boaters and walkers alike.

*ABOVE: Houghton's 17th-century mill is now a National Trust property with milling on Sundays and Bank Holiday Mondays.*

# CAVENDISH

## SUFFOLK

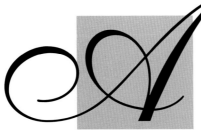

A pretty group of pink-washed thatched cottages stands at the back of a large green with an imposing flint church glittering behind them. It is a scene captured countless times by artists and photographers, and, it seems, one of which we shall never grow tired. With a thatched pub, red-brick Victorian school and timber-framed manor house almost within the same view, it is a vista that appears to embody all those qualities we value most in our English villages: tranquility, continuity, stability.

But appearances can be deceptive. Within living memory, the high street was an unmetalled lane running through the village from Clare to Long Melford, and sheep grazed freely across the green. The well-known 'Hyde Park Corner' cottages have been rebuilt twice since they were first constructed in the 16th century. The most recent occasion was after a devastating fire in 1971, a mere 13 years after extensive renovation by the Cavendish Preservation Society.

The Five Bells pub is also a 20th-century structure, erected on the site of an old thatched hostelry of the same name, while the lovely Nether Hall is a 15th-century replacement of an earlier building; through the ages, the hall has been manor house, farmhouse and most recently the office of Cavendish Manor Vineyards. In 1381, the medieval church was caught up in the aftermath of the Peasants' Revolt when news reached the village that the son of local nobleman, Sir John Cavendish, had played a part in the death of Wat Tyler. An enraged mob went in search of the father who, fearing for his life, fled to the door of St Mary's Church and clung to the iron ring of its handle, claiming sanctuary. Any asylum he may have been given was short-lived, for he was dragged to a mock trial at the market cross in Bury St Edmunds and beheaded. The 650-year-old church door, with its original iron handle is still in place, while a bequest of £40 in Sir John's will paid for the chancel that we see today.

There are many fine survivors from Cavendish's past as a wealthy medieval 'wool' village, which add both visual and historical interest today. The Sue Ryder Foundation now owns the 16th-century Old Rectory and has turned it into a museum of the Holocaust, while close by ducks still frequent the attractive, though somewhat reduced, pond. A charming old house with raised pargeting in the form of a Tudor rose was at one time a private school, while the Elizabethan grammar school was partly demolished to make way for a cinema. Nearby, a three-gabled property, formerly the Cavendish Institute and Reading Rooms, once belonged to the Cavendish family whose ancestral village this is. Later to become the Dukes of Devonshire, they are perhaps better known as the lords of the Chatsworth estate in Derbyshire.

Strolling through this beautifully kept village on a warm summer afternoon, it is difficult to equate it with the place described in the mid-19th century as damp, muddy, filthy and one of the unhealthiest places to live in the area. Lying on the northern bank of the River Stour, only marginally above its general flood level, the village's low-lying houses and roads were frequently flooded. One doctor who had worked in the region for 20 years declared that he 'met more fever there than anywhere else'. The situation is very different today, of course, and property in the lovely village of Cavendish has become highly sought-after.

*RIGHT: The 14th century tower of St Mary's rises behind the famous huddle of cottages at 'Hyde Park Corner' - so-called because visiting preachers would always choose this corner of the green for their soap box.*

# KERSEY

## SUFFOLK

**K**ersey's long and picturesque main street dips down into the watersplash of its ford before sweeping up once more to a fine medieval church, which enjoys a prominent hilltop position above the village. On either side range Tudor merchants' houses of ancient timbers and weathered brick, together with weavers' cottages leaning heavily on their centuries-old timber frames. The latter paint a delightful picture with their irregular angles and colourful walls beneath roofs of thatch or pantile.

Here, a tributary of the River Brett – little more than a brook – trickles through a small notch of a valley. Rather than following the water's course, the village has straddled it with buildings close by on either side that channel its flow. Since 1490, the magnificent red brick River House has stood securely behind its great oak door at the fording place, the little brook running alongside. This ancient building will have witnessed the cleansing of wool at the water's edge and the splashing hoofs of countless pack animals. Some of the beasts may have stopped to drink before wending their weary way uphill and downhill, to and from the weaver's cottages, delivering the raw materials and carrying forth the finished fabric.

A prosperous and well known textile town in the Middle Ages, Kersey gave its name to the cloth produced here, and both found fame in the works of Shakespeare. Kersey cloth was coarse, ribbed, hard-wearing and a good insulator against the cold and wet. It was much in demand across Europe and at home and as a result, almost every building in Kersey speaks of the prosperity of times past, but perhaps none more so than St Mary's. It is a large and beautifully decorated church whose rich craftsmanship could not be obscured by the hands of either 17th-century Puritan 'wreckers' or 19th-century restorers. It stands proudly on its hilltop, while at the opposite end of the village in an equally lofty position lie the ruins of a great 12th-century Augustinian priory, the remnants of its great church obscured by the trees and undergrowth to the east of Priory Farm.

As the local wool industry wound down towards the end of the 17th century, Kersey turned to agriculture, and, despite the problems faced by that industry, the village has survived virtually intact. Today, Kersey is still surrounded by arable farmland, although few villagers work on the land. The tiny village school can be found behind the church and one wonderful old pub remains: the magnificently black-and-white half-timbered Bell inn, which has stood beside Kersey's main street since the 14th century. A wooden-clad pump by the former 16th-century White Horse inn (now a private residence) at the northern end of the village provided fresh water for the abstemious.

However, the marketplace has long been nothing more than a particularly wide road junction, while the shops and businesses that thrived here within living memory have all closed. There is no longer a village store or post office although a row of stables has been converted into a most successful pottery (with its own studio shop) that produces high-quality items from local materials, popular with the many coach parties that stop here each summer to admire and photograph Kersey's delightful thatched porches and crooked half-timbered walls.

*RIGHT: One of the oldest buildings in the village River House has stood beside Kersey's famous ford for more than 500 years. The name of the village means 'island where cress grows' (Cærsige c995 AD).*

# MONKS ELEIGH

## SUFFOLK

**M**onks Eleigh is a delightful confection of prettily gabled and dormered, cream-washed or 'Suffolk pink' cottages, interspersed with splashes of primrose yellow and cornflower blue. The village sign and mid-Victorian pump stand on a neat triangular green that leads away from the busy main road and up a small hill to the peaceful enclave of school, hall and church at the top.

An avenue of pollarded limes shelters the approach to the lofty church of St Peter. Its tall 15th-century tower, visible from a considerable distance away, has lost its old wooden spire; the unhoused clock bell can be seen atop the projecting stair turret. Inside, an ornately carved cover dating from the 15th century sits atop a 13th-century stone font and a large painting of the Royal Arms of Queen Anne, from 1705, still hangs above the chancel arch

Monks Eleigh, set alongside the River Brett, was once one of the great wool-producing villages of the Brett valley. Situated just 5km (3 miles) from Lavenham and 6.5km (4 miles) from Kersey (see page 102), it lies in an area that used to be one of

OPPOSITE: *The village estate was gifted to Canterbury by the widow of Ealdorman Brythnoth in AD 991*

BELOW: *Prosperity in Monks Eleigh reached a peak in the 16th century. Much of its architecture dates from this time.*

the busiest and wealthiest places in England. Tangible evidence of the village's prosperity at that time can be found in the form of a handsome 14th-century thatched and cream-washed pub and restaurant: The Swan. But foreign wars, changes in fashion and later technical innovations were to wreck the economy of many of Suffolk's textile villages, while those that survived, such as Monks Eleigh, were eventually reduced to spinning yarn for production centres elsewhere.

Sophisticated as the village community had become, the exploitation of old superstitions by new grudges continued. In December 1748, the parish register reported that Alice, the wife of a labourer called Thomas Green, was 'swam, malicious and evil, people having raised an ill-report of her for being a witch'. 'Swimming' had been used as a means of detecting the agents of the devil for centuries, despite the fact that, perversely, it often resulted in the death of those deemed innocent.

One old village tradition it would be hard to disapprove of, for all its pagan associations, is the making of corn dollies. A local craft centre grows and hand-reaps its own crop of special wheat for that very purpose. Yet while the craft centre is doing well and looking to expand, the old post office in the main street was forced to close. Determined not to see the loss of such a service signal the beginning of the end for a lively community that could still boast a thriving school, local residents joined together to form the Monks Eleigh Community Shop Association. Hard work and perseverance were rewarded at last in February 2004, when a new shop and post office opened.

# BLAKENEY

## NORFOLK

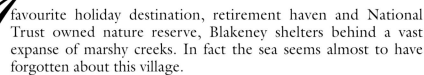favourite holiday destination, retirement haven and National Trust owned nature reserve, Blakeney shelters behind a vast expanse of marshy creeks. In fact the sea seems almost to have forgotten about this village.

Yet on the evening of Saturday January 31 1953, the sea made a dramatic return to Blakeney. During the worst storm in the North Sea for centuries, a massive wall of water was hurled along the eastern coast of Britain. Hundreds lost their lives that night as freezing floodwater engulfed the lowest-lying homes, while terrified survivors clung to rooftops in gale force winds, praying for rescue. Blakeney was lucky: there were no fatalities among its villagers. Although many had lost all that they possessed, everyone was simply thankful that they had come through the disaster alive.

Blakeney's history has always been shaped by the forces of nature, albeit generally in a far less dramatic fashion. For centuries, a series of offshore sandbars created a shel-

tered haven, but since the mid-19th century longshore drift and deposition in the estuary of the River Glaven have transformed them into a shifting spit of sand and shingle that is moving landward at the rate of 1 metre (3.3 feet) a year. Coupled with the advent of the railways and the construction of ever-larger vessels, the effects upon this once-busy medieval port have been devastating.

Already an important fishing and trading port, Blakeney gained its market charter in 1222. In the century that followed a house of Carmelite friars was established there. They would bless seagoing expeditions from a chapel on the quayside. A reminder of those prosperous times can be found in the remains of a 14th-century merchant's house known as Blakeney Guildhall (now owned by English Heritage) that shelters at the foot of the hill overlooking the broad quay. Throughout the 16th and 17th centuries, imports of coal, iron, timber

and Flemish bricks and tiles would have swapped places across the quayside with north Norfolk's major exports of wool and cereal crops; while The Crown and Anchor inn, demolished in 1921 when the Blakeney Hotel was constructed, was reputed to have been the favourite haunt of smugglers; there are many tales of mysterious tunnels running between various properties in the village. But over time the workings of tide and river meant that the harbour grew ever shallower, and by the early 20th century, all trade there had ceased.

Blakeney's steep high street climbs away from the bracing salt breezes of the seafront. Along its length can be found numerous sheltered, sun-drenched courts and alleys leading to delightful gardens and hidden yards. At the top of the hill a slender tower rises from the chancel of the Church of St Nicholas; it once served as a beacon for the hundreds of ships that sought the port of Blakeney.

*OPPOSITE: Blakeney is a fascinating mix of flint-pebble fishermen's cottages and larger merchants' houses of warm red brick.*

*BELOW: Now a sleepy seaside village on the north Norfolk coast Blakeney's quayside is often crowded with small pleasure craft.*

# GODWICK
*the story of a deserted village*

## NORFOLK

nglish villages have proved remarkably resilient over the last 1,000 years. Wars and raids have seen many burned to the ground, but the villagers who fled would return and rebuild. Only in extreme circumstances, such as William the Conqueror's 'Harrying of the North', when an entire region was laid waste and its population annihilated, would such destruction prove fatal to a settlement. Even then, a prime location would not have remained uninhabited for long.

Later, in the 14th century, when the Black Death wiped out more than a third of the country's population, many communities were pushed to the brink of extinction. However, in the end few failed solely because of the plague. The exhaustion of the soil through overfarming driven by population pressure and long periods of cold damp weather, affected all communities, but only those already on the edge, struggling to win a living from poorer marginal lands, did not survive.

Villagers everywhere, no matter how viable their community, were helpless in the face of natural forces such as coastal erosion, silting or deposition, sand blows, or the increased incidence of flooding. Yet the destructive acts of man were just as devastating, and possibly more frequent. If a village managed to survive the Norman proclivity for vast hunting grounds, the creation of deer parks and the monasteries' consolidation of their endowments and gifts, it would still have to face sweeping changes in agricultural practice, including the medieval shift from arable farming to huge sheep walks and the 17th-century aesthetic embellishment of grand country estates. More recently, the formation of reservoirs and the establishment of army training ranges have also been responsible for forcibly removing entire communities from their villages.

Wharram Percy, in Yorkshire, is perhaps the country's most famous deserted medieval village. Despite decades of excavation and careful research, the reasons for its abandonment remain unclear. Godwick in Norfolk, on the other hand, almost certainly succumbed to deteriorating climatic conditions in the 16th century. Traces remain of a series of rectangular medieval house plots either side of a broad main street, while to the east there is evidence that a dam once held back a millpond for a small mill. The village was built on sticky boulder clay and the ground became increasingly unworkable as the weather worsened, until by 1596 successive bad harvests and a dwindling population saw the once-thriving Saxon village reduced to a mere handful of houses beside a church whose 13th-century tower was crumbling.

Edward Coke, the Chief Justice and Attorney General of Elizabeth I, had purchased the estate in 1580 and quickly built a fine brick manor house, complete with walled yard and formal gardens, amid the decaying remains of the village. An elaborate brick barn was constructed across the line of the main street. The church was eventually demolished in the 17th century, but the tower was built up as a folly and remains to this day, as does the barn, although the Coke mansion was pulled down in the 1960s. Now managed by English Heritage under an agreement with the landowner, who is determined to see the site preserved for future generations, Godwick is not only a pleasant – if somewhat melancholy – excursion into the past, but also a valuable educational resource.

*RIGHT: Norfolk has more than 200 known abandoned village sites, of which Godwick is probably the best preserved. Often referred to as Deserted Medieval Villages (DMVs), such sites are by no means exclusively medieval.*

# WOODBASTWICK

## NORFOLK

Wonderfully carved pictorial signs depicting a real or legendary scene from a community's history are especially popular in Norfolk, and those seeking an explanation for the name of this pretty little estate village need only to look at its sign. It shows an early settler tying his leggings with cord manufactured from bast, the fibrous material found beneath the bark of the lime tree, one of which is about to be felled by his axe-wielding companion. Woodbastwick means 'farm where bast can be obtained'.

The extraction and processing of bast is thought to have been introduced into the country by Germanic settlers, though many believe it was specifically the Danish Vikings who first exploited the versatile bast resources at Woodbastwick to make rope, cord, mats and baskets. If this is true, then the Vikings might claim much of the credit for both the village's origins and its continuing existence. Today, Woodbastick is known throughout the world as the home of the British White breed of cattle. These were originally introduced in small numbers by traders or invaders from Scandinavia in the

8th century. Nine hundred years later, the park of Whalley Abbey in the Forest of Bowland, owned by the Assheton family, could boast a large herd of the animals.

When Mary Assheton married Sir Harbord Harbord (later Lord Suffield) of Gunton, Norfolk, in 1760, it is thought that she brought some of these cattle with her. In 1840, the fourth Lord Suffield sold some animals from the herd founded on this stock to Albemarle Cator of Woodbastwick Hall who went on to breed a substantial herd of his own. There have been British White cattle at Woodbastwick ever since, and it is largely through the efforts and expertise of the Cator family (who still own and manage the estate) that the breed continues to thrive today.

Thatch is everywhere in Woodbastwick, from its picturesque cottages dating from the 18th century onwards, to the well at the centre of the green, its mechanism sheltering beneath a wonderful thatched roof. Even the captivating little church with its elegant pinnacled tower, and elaborately tiled lychgate, has a thatched nave.

Woodbastwick today is a peaceful village lying within The Broads National Park, and alongside the River Bure. The school closed in the 1970s, when only three pupils remained on its books, and now the village population consists mainly of farmworkers, both employed and retired. There is no shop, although the post office at nearby Salhouse can meet most immediate requirements, while the village pub is a recent development and something of a surprise. Called the Fur and Feather inn and situated beside a pretty pond, it is in fact a pair of old farm cottages converted into a brewery tap, for behind them lies Woodforde's award-winning Broadland Brewery which opened in 1989 and now employs more than 20 people. Nearby, Woodbastwick's 17th-century forge, long disused and in poor repair, has been lovingly restored. Here, the blacksmith forges anything from fireside pokers to bishops' crooks.

*OPPOSITE:*
*One cottage has a quotation from Zaccharia 14:7 painted in white along one of its blackened timbers: 'At evening-time it shall be light'.*

*BELOW: With a thatched well-house in its centre and the church of SS Fabian and Sebastian rising behind the green at Woodbastwick must be among the most photographed in Norfolk.*

# BRACEBY

## LINCOLNSHIRE

raceby has a different face in every season: so dominant are the enclosing trees and hedges that as they change through the year the whole aspect of the village alters. A small settlement typical of the Kesteven Uplands within which it lies the village is set in an elevated position 11km (7 miles) east of Grantham and 1.5km (1 mile) from the A52.

Now peaceful and relatively isolated, Braceby would have been busy in Roman times, with nearby villas and settlements connected by lanes that wound through the surrounding woodland. Neighbouring Sapperton, which lay on Ermine Street only 6.5km (4 miles) away, was the site for a Roman town, while Braceby grew alongside a connecting road between Bourne and the fort at Ancaster, its northern boundary marked by the forerunner of the A52, then a much-used salter's road from the fens.

As a small farming community, Braceby has left little evidence of its early years. Referred to as Brezbi in the Domesday Book, its name betrays Danish influence, while its site was chosen perhaps because of the abundance of freshwater wells in the vicinity.

By the 13th century, the village had gained a beautiful little church. Sharing a rector with Sapperton, St Margaret's was a chapel of Grantham, its dimensions expanding and contracting according to changing attitudes towards religion as well as the fluctuating fortunes of the village.

At its largest in the 19th century, Braceby had nearly 40 houses for a population of more than 160. There were three large farms together with many independent smallholdings and the village had its own shop and school as well as a smithy and a carpenter. However, as increased mechanization in farming led to a decrease in demand for farm workers, people gradually moved away. Ropsley's village school eventually took over the education of Braceby's children and post-war rationing in the 1950s led to the demise of the shop, although previously 'roundsmen' had carried on much trade in the village, with bakers, butchers and greengrocers selling their wares door to door.

Braceby's small village green once sat at the intersection of two roads, but now finds itself perched on the outer corner of a bend in the one main street that curves sharply through the village. While the green is centrally placed, the buildings of the village do not surround it. Instead, they cluster in three groups around Manor, College, and Church farms. Many are Grade II-listed properties dating from the 17th century; all built of local limestone ashlar or coursed rubble, their thatched roofs have been replaced by pantiles.

Today, the land in the village is owned by the Welby estate, which controls all but 14 acres. As the new acquisitions were consolidated within the existing farm structure, many disused farm buildings and cottages were demolished. Consequently Braceby has become a tiny hamlet of less than a dozen dwellings. While the village was designated a Conservation Area by South Kesteven District Council in 2000, new buildings are not prohibited, and so it may be that all of Braceby's story has not yet been told.

*OPPOSITE: Braceby's Manor Farm, the only remaining working farm in the village, was built with local limestone in the 17th century but has been lengthened and remodelled since.*

*BELOW: Parts of College Farm may be the oldest structures in the village. Once the property of Corpus Christi, Oxford, it appears in a 1609 survey of college holdings.*

# CASTLE BYTHAM

## LINCOLNSHIRE

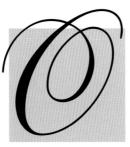do, half-brother to William the Conqueror, completed the great stronghold at Bytham began by the vanquished and imprisoned Saxon Earl Morcar, brother of the dead king Harold. The name 'castle' was duly added to that of the settlement that prospered at its gates, and the castle stood for 150 years upon its impressive earthworks until besieged by Henry III in 1221. Its replacement, raised by William de Colville, fared no better, being destroyed by fire during the Wars of the Roses. However, some parts of the fortress survived until the late 18th century when the demand for good-quality building materials saw the castle ruins plundered to nothing.

Today, Castle Bytham is an attractive hillside village. Its stone cottages clamber diagonally up the steep incline from castle to church either side of a small triangular green, also lining its upper edge, along a lateral road that skirts the foot of a limestone ridge. Although only 6.5km (4 miles) from the thundering A1, Castle Bytham enjoys pleasant seclusion, despite being hailed by many as the best village in the county. Its pretty pantile roofs in red or yellow sit above mellow stone dwellings that give little away about their age. Yet there are houses here whose blackened roof timbers lead on to a search for inserted floors and the stone supports for screen passages put in place

*RIGHT: There are two old pubs in Castle Bytham; The Castle inn, and the Fox and Hounds.*

*MIDDLE: On rising ground above the village, the 12th-century Church of St James sits amid dark yews in its secluded churchyard.*

during the Middle Ages, for they were once open halls. Priory House by the church is one such structure.

The manor house dates from the 17th century – a time of upheaval and revolution in the land. For a period of 11 years, England was a republican state ruled by a Puritan elite who saw it as their duty to rid the churches of their former idolatrous ways and to forbid all merrymaking that could be construed as pagan in origin. The traditional May celebrations were one such casualty, although many defied the edicts and erected maypoles as a show of defiance. After years of oppression, it is hardly surprising that at the Restoration in 1660 there was unrestrained merriment. Castle Bytham retains a relic of this time: in a corner of the Norman nave of the 12th-century church of St James is propped a ladder, once used to reach the belfry, which proclaims: 'This ware the May Poul 1660'.

The church is reached by a narrow pathway called Church Lane, which winds upwards through deep shade, with the shadowy churchyard to one side. On the south face of the tower is an 18th-century sundial, which bears a comic play on words: 'Bee in Thyme'. A little further on is the old school, tucked away in a shady corner; its date stone reads 1907.

The Old Bakehouse is a wonderfully warm, biscuity building in Heathcote Road. Running down one side of the green from the High Street almost to the duck pond at the bottom of the hill, this short road was named after a family who were once lords of the manor here. Beginning in the 18th century, the Heathcotes built up their holdings in the village by buying out the smaller landowners until, by the mid-19th century, they owned nearly 1,300 acres of land, both pubs, the post office and the lime quarry, as well as numerous cottages and farms. But when Robert Heathcote died in 1917, the estate was sold off in lots at auction, and now most of the village is owner-occupied.

*ABOVE: Since 1973, Castle Bytham has enjoyed the protection of being an officially designated conservation area within the South Kesteven district of Lincolnshire. The name Bytham comes from the Old English 'bythme' which means 'valley bottom'.*

# EXTON

## RUTLAND

*I*n the early 16th century, the village of Exton passed through marriage from the Brus family, who had held it since the Norman Conquest, into the hands of the Haringtons. A powerful force in Rutland, the family reached the zenith of its influence when Sir John Harington was made a baron at the coronation of James I. However, increased status had its drawbacks. Entrusted with the guardianship of the young princess Elizabeth Stuart, Harington soon found that entertaining royalty could be an expensive business. In 1613, he was freed from his duty when his charge married Frederick the Elector Palatine (Elizabeth eventually became Queen of Bohemia), but poor Sir John died on his way home from the wedding and his estate was sold to pay his creditors.

Sir Baptist Hicks, a wealthy London businessman, became the next owner of the Exton estate, although his eldest daughter Julia took possession of the hall upon her marriage into the noble Noel family, and it has remained with them ever since. Badly damaged by fire in 1810, the fine Elizabethan hall is now a romantic ruin. At the end of Pudding Bag Lane, Exton's new hall, completed in 1852, is based around the large farmhouse to which the Noels removed after the catastrophe, while stone from the ruins of their former residence was later used to build a Catholic church alongside their new home.

The parish church of St Peter and St Paul, on the other hand, dates from the 13th and 14th centuries. Struck by lightning in 1843, it suffered such severe damage that extensive rebuilding was necessary, but thankfully the monuments inside, including a rare marble by master woodcarver Grinling Gibbons, were spared. The remainder of this amber ironstone and grey-buff limestone village is 16th century or later. Many of the cottages are thatched, some most decoratively, while others are very plain. Built on a slope, they sit individually in neat garden plots or are ranged in attractive terraces, such as the picturesque row in Blacksmith's Lane with its crooked line of dormers.

At one corner of the sycamore-studded green stands the village's only remaining pub. While several houses in Exton retain cellars that reveal their former incarnations as alehouses, the Fox and Hounds occupies a large and impressive building, similar in character to the other handsome houses that surround the green. Nearby is School Yard, the site of Exton's Church of England school; during the 19th century, Catholic children were educated separately at St Mary's at the top of the High Street. Amalgamated in 1967, the newly formed school also occupies a brand new site in Garden Road to the east of the village.

The village pump beneath its conical stone roof, once the only source of drinking water in the village, was rendered superfluous at the beginning of the 20th century, when standpipes were installed (it has since been removed although its shelter remains). Gone too are the Methodist chapel, nursing home, gasworks and workhouse, while in 1960, Old Horse Pond on Oakham Road was filled in. At one time there was a blacksmith, butcher, fishmonger and baker in the village, but no more, and the United Steel Company's ironstone quarry closed in 1974. But stand on the sun-dappled green with the scent of wood smoke in the air and nothing but the sound of birdsong to break the silence, and suddenly Exton seems quite the most perfect place to live.

*RIGHT: This handsome village can boast many picturesque thatched cottages. Exton means 'ox farm', but the estate is perhaps better known for having been Rutland's largest park, roamed by a herd of around 500 deer.*

# Central England and the

To speak of the Midlands is often to conjure pictures of a ravaged landscape irrevocably scarred by more than two centuries of industrialization, while to speak of the Welsh Marches will most frequently engender blank expressions. Yet mention the names Herefordshire, Worcestershire, Warwickshire, Shropshire and Cheshire, and immediately stares of incomprehension are replaced by warm smiles, no doubt prompted by mental images of lush farmland, fine brown cattle and

# West

*dazzling 'magpie' houses of blackened timbers and white plaster or colour-washed brick.*

*From the foothills of the Welsh mountains to the flooded opencast iron workings of Rutland, this is a region rich in romance and local colour. For while it is true that much of the centre and east of the region is best known for the extraction of coal, lead and iron, as well as being the birthplace of mass production, who could deny the stern beauty of the mountains and wild moors of the Peak Distict, the shining meres of Shropshire, or the timeless quality of Leicestershire's Charnwood Forest, seemingly unchanged for millennia.*

*As for the settlements, there is a subtle, dignified charm to the remote grey-stone villages and peg-toothed drystone walls of Derbyshire and Staffordshire, not to mention the sober slate of Leicestershire, Nottinghamshire's fine houses of grey lias limestone, the vibrant red sandstone of Shropshire, and the rusty ironstone of Rutland.*

*LEFT: In Eardisland, Herefordshire, wide lawns and attractive houses line the banks of the River Arrow and its parallel mill-race. Eardisland is one of a number of attractive black-and-white villages richly endowed with ancient timber-framed properties for which the county is justly famous.*

# EARDISLAND

## HEREFORDSHIRE

*I*n 1902, the vicar of Eardisland discovered from the parish registers that in the previous 124 years no fewer than 38 parishioners had surpassed their allotted 'three score years and ten'. Perhaps his investigation had been prompted by the tale of 'Widow Hill' who was said to have been 111 when she died in 1676, or perhaps it was the earlier 1609 report of 'Old Meg', the famous Wench of Eardisland, believed to have managed nine years more. Looking at Eardisland, often voted 'Prettiest Village in the Midlands', it is easy to understand their reluctance to go!

The origins of Eardisland are only just beginning to be understood, but it is thought that the first wooden houses here were clustered around the moat of a timber Saxon stronghold erected on a site behind the present church. Possibly built to guard the fording place of an important route between England and Wales, it would also have served as a refuge for villagers and their livestock in the event of an attack.

Today the focal point of this most enchanting of north Herefordshire's 'black-and-white villages' is undoubtedly the area around the bridge over the River Arrow. Contrary to popular belief, the Arrow is as prone to overflowing its banks as any other river in the county, and the lovely lawns and gardens that line its course (and that of the parallel mill race) have found themselves submerged countless times in the past. Happily, most of the time the Arrow singularly fails to live up to the implied dynamism of its name. Instead, it flows placidly past a delightful collection of 16th-century timber and plaster cottages, their somewhat eccentric arrangement thought to be the result of each one standing within its own original medieval croft.

At one end of the bridge stands an imposing 17th-century dovecote once owned by the lord of the manor. The birds it housed would have provided a convenient supply of fresh meat in the winter, but when farming methods changed in the 18th century, Eardisland's unusual example was left to decay. It was saved through the efforts of the Eardisland Millennium Fund and is now a heritage centre. Indeed, so successful had the fundraising been that the surplus was used to restore a 1920s AA (Automobile Association) telephone box, thought to be the only surviving specimen in the country. It stands beside the war memorial in a little white-railed garden near the Cross inn.

Opposite the inn stands the grand 17th-century manor house with its incongruous Queen Anne brick extension, and nearby can be found Knapp House, a cruck-framed hall put up sometime at the beginning of the 15th century. Even older, the large timber-framed Staick House, located on the riverbank north of the bridge, once served as the vicarage. This wonderful old yeoman's house, now sagging beneath its heavy roof of stone tiles, has been extended over the centuries, its oldest part being early 14th-century, its newest 17th-century.

Below the southern parapet of the bridge, Millstream Cottage, built in 1652, was formerly the old school. At one time the proceeds from concerts featuring amateur performers from the village paid for each of the schoolchildren to enjoy a daily cup of hot cocoa, as many ate little or nothing during school hours. Eardisland's school closed in 1979, by which time the register held only 20 names where once there had been more than 100, but the 'cocoa concerts' are still remembered fondly in the village.

*RIGHT: Eardisland's splendid 17th-century red-brick dovecote has been converted into a heritage centre. It stands on the south bank of the mill-race which flows beneath the interesting Mill Cottage although the mill itself no longer stands.*

# WEOBLEY

## HEREFORDSHIRE

A dazzling masterpiece of eccentric geometry, Weobley (pronounced 'Webley') provides a rare opportunity to view at first hand the development of timber-frame construction. Within the space of only a few streets it is possible to trace the progression from cruck frames, incorporating split trees, to the more economical and flexible box-frame method that employed timber uprights, known as studs, reinforced by horizontal beams, and to note the way these studs were placed progressively further apart as timber became increasingly scarce.

'Redevelopment' in the 19th-century saw the demolition of as many as 40 buildings within the village including the old town hall, thought to have been the work of John Abel – a master builder and a leading craftsman of his day – which went in 1860. Further losses occurred in 1943 when a fire tore through the old market area, rendering Broad Street somewhat broader than before. A walled garden now marks the site of the destruction.

Local man, Benjamin Tomkins, is credited with the creation of the famous Hereford breed of red-and-white beef cattle at Weobley in the late 18th century. Less than a 100 years later a directory of Herefordshire proclaimed: 'This is an exceedingly fertile and productive district; the scenes around are most picturesque and romantic'. No doubt the Normans once thought so too, because they built a castle here to defend the Marcher barony of Weobley against attack by the Welsh. In 1135, it was garrisoned on behalf of the Empress Matilda, but was taken by her brother, King Stephen, in the civil war. When John Leland, Henry VIII's topographer, visited Weobley 400 years later, he described it as 'a goodly castell but somewhat in decay'. Only the earthworks are visible today, to the south of the village.

Also dating from Norman times is the church of St Peter and St Paul, which was extensively remodelled in the 14th century, at around the time that the Red Lion was built in Bell Square. Behind this pub is an old cruck barn converted into a cottage, which, it is claimed, is the oldest in England. Weobley's Unicorn Hotel is another of John Abel's masterful late 17th-century creations, while a farmhouse situated beside the Hereford

OPPOSITE: *Weobley's elegant church spire rises behind the superb black-and-white Red Lion built in the 14th century.*

BELOW: *Not all of Weobley's fine timber-framed buildings are black and white; several have colour-washed infill panels.*

Road and called The Throne, was once the original Unicorn Inn. It was renamed after the battle of Naseby in 1645 when Charles I took shelter there for the night. Just outside the village, The Ley (a wonderful 16th-century structure) has the reputation of being the most beautiful timber-framed farmhouse in Herefordshire.

Fine buildings on such a scale would not have been possible without substantial financial foundations. During the Middle Ages, the popular 'Weobley Ale' and a thriving glove-making industry provided such a boost to the economy of this otherwise agricultural village that it was granted borough status. Later, Colonel John Birch of nearby Garnstone House, a one-time Bristol merchant and former Parliamentary commander in the English Civil Wars, did much to improve conditions in the village, albeit in an attempt to win votes, for he coveted one of Weobley's two parliamentary seats. This was not an easy task considering that the village had been staunchly Royalist and that Birch was best known in the area for having seized the nearby city of Hereford for Oliver Cromwell.

Weobley's status as a 'rotten', or 'pocket', borough was not challenged until 1832, when the Reform Act saw it disenfranchized. Gone, too, are the annual May Fair, for the trading of cattle and hiring of labour, and the Weobley hunt and steeple chase, which was once held on a local farm every April. Today, Weobley's transformation back into a village is complete and the residents could not be more proud: with its well-kept streets, fine shops, welcoming inns and strong community spirit, Weobley has won the prestigious 'Village of the Year' competition twice in succession.

# OMBERSLEY
## WORCESTERSHIRE

*A*t the point where the Droitwich road crosses the old turnpike from Kidderminster to Worcester, an attractive village has grown along three of the approaches. Were it not for the A449 bypass skirting its eastern edge, it would no doubt be eyeing the fourth. While the centre of Ombersley is now a rather uninspiring round-about amid much modern development, venture south along the road towards Worcester and you will be rewarded with a glimpse of how things were here in times past.

A bold accumulation of various architectural styles and dimensions, Ombersley's interesting main street of mellow brick and traditional black-and-white is probably quieter now than it has been for many hundreds of years, following the opening of the much-needed bypass in 1976. In the great turnpike era of the 18th century, this street

*RIGHT: The timber-framed Kings Arms is one of 20 buildings in the village listed as of special historic or architectural interest. Many fine and decorative black-and-white properties line the former Worcester to Kidderminster turn-pike road.*

would have reverberated with the oaths of coachmen, the din of rumbling iron-bound wheels creaking coachwork, and jingling harnesses.

The Kings Arms public house, with its bowed black-and-white timbered end leaning proudly into the street, would have seen all this and more. Its first timbers were put up in 1411, but the structure has been added to over the centuries as its owners – and the village – prospered. Inside the pub, the visitor finds an evocative scene of oak beams and flagstone floors. By contrast, only a short distance up the street the large Crown and Sandys Arms stands like a curiously gabled block of vanilla ice cream, its new brick orangery pushing itself forward as if to be noticed.

The latter inn is named in honour of the great Sandys family. Descended from kings of Scotland they succeeded the

Abbots of Evesham as owners of Ombersley in the mid-16th century. With only a brief (forced) intermission, they have been here ever since. Sir Samuel Sandys was responsible for much of Ombersley's finest black-and-white architecture from the late 16th and early 17th centuries. His brother, Edwin, was a patron of the Pilgrim Fathers, while another brother, George, was himself a leading Virginia planter and wrote the colony's constitution - said to have been used by George Washington as the blueprint for the American Constitution. A later Samuel Sandys began the building of Ombersley Court, a fine Queen Anne mansion that stands in landscaped grounds on the edge of the village; a replacement for the manor house that had been burnt to the ground following the capture of yet another Samuel who had been a Royalist commander during the English Civil Wars.

Perhaps as early as the 8th century AD the road through Ombersley would have been a source of revenue for the villagers. Yet, steady through traffic could bring disaster as well as prosperity. In 1348, a plague swept through the country, so devastating that it became known as the Black Death. Ombersley retains a reminder of those desperate times in the form of a hollowed out slab of rock called a 'plague stone'. Placed at the roadside on the outskirts of the village, those tradesmen too terrified to enter the stricken place would leave their goods by the stone, within which they would find payment, the coins drenched in vinegar as a precaution against infection.

Ombersley also has many reminders of more prosperous times, during which its market thrived and its back lanes and alleyways led to wonderful apple orchards. In those days, it enjoyed a confidence born from centuries of relative stability under the benevolent stewardship of the Sandys. Smart businesses still line the main street, for the benefit of local people and the occasional traveller alike: establishments whose pursuit of excellence is a quality that pervades the whole village and which looks certain to ensure continued success.

# ELMLEY CASTLE
## WORCESTERSHIRE

In the 8th century AD, there was no 'castle' in the name of this wonderful old village because it had yet to be built. In those days, it was simply Elmlege, or 'the clearing in the elm tree wood'. By 1327, when the castle finally made an appearance in the written record, the structure itself was already in an advanced state of decay, and today barely a trace of it remains.

A Norman fortification built at the time Domesday and situated high above the village on an outcrop of Bredon Hill's north-east slope, the castle passed through marriage to the Beauchamp family. Absentee lords at first, they were to retreat there during the civil war of 1135 as they were supporters of the ultimately vanquished Empress Matilda in her struggle against her sibling Stephen for the English throne. The presence of such a great family brought prosperity to the tiny village, but when their fortunes recovered and the Beauchamps became greater still, they removed to Warwick Castle in 1269. Elmley Castle, now abandoned, fell into disrepair.

It remained thus for nearly 50 years under three different monarchs, until, fearful of rebellion, Edward II dispatched commissioners to assess the state of readiness of all

castles in his kingdom. Their verdict on the derelict stronghold at Elmley was that it was worth only six shillings and sixpence! Dismayed, the king sent a second party of commissioners to double-check the work of the first, but these concluded that things were even worse than initially reported and declared it worthless. Undeterred, Edward had the stronghold refortified and employment prospects for the villagers in its shadow were immeasurably improved. Yet when the uprising finally came, Elmley fell quickly. Ultimately, however, the rebellion failed and the battered castle was returned to the Crown.

In 1575, Elizabeth I visited the Savage family, who resided in Elmley at that time. Such events were often ruinously expensive for the queen's hosts and, although the royal guest is proudly commemorated in the name of a fine Tudor hostelry to one side of the enchanting little village square, perhaps the strain of Her Majesty's progress proved too much for the small community. Its castle soon reverted to a ruinous state, the walls plundered for building stone and the prosperity of the settlement declined steadily.

Across the upper end of the picturesque main street stretch the gates of St Mary's Church, almost lost amid the trees in its vast churchyard. Built in the 11th century, its simple exterior hides treasures within. A pretty tree-lined brook follows the edge of the road and all around are delightful cottages, some of them thatched, many of them half-timbered and surrounded by enchanting little gardens. Happily, modern housing has been integrated so sensitively with the old that Elmley Castle looks set to enjoy many more years of being described as one of the loveliest villages in England.

# HONINGTON

## WARWICKSHIRE

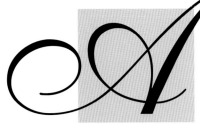

*BELOW: Pretty as a picture, this almost too perfect former estate village once served successive owners of Honington Hall.*

*A*s you turn off the main road and pass between two impressive gateless piers topped with stone pineapples (a symbol of welcome), you enter what was once a private estate. So private and secluded are your surroundings that it is difficult not to feel that perhaps you have made a wrong turn, that maybe you are not meant to be there. This feeling intensifies as you cross open parkland and traverse the odd little 17th-century bridge, decorated with umpteen stone globes, that spans the River Stour. Yet there before you lies Honington village, known as Hunitone in the Domesday Book, or 'the farmstead where honey is produced'.

Life here certainly seems sweet. Honington is, as it has frequently been described in the past, 'exceptionally pretty', and it displays an almost surreal neatness. It is easy to see why it has often won the title of Warwickshire's Best Kept Village: it is truly immaculate and ready for the judges to pay a visit at any time. What may once have been a traditional village green has been divided by lanes and paths into what

RIGHT: *Honington feels very much an enclosed community, its secluded setting lending it an air of supreme tranquility.*

amounts to a series of exceptionally wide verges. Yet the abundant grass here is like plush, well vacuumed carpet, and behind it, sitting in orderly gardens, are trim brick and stone dwellings, some built around a timber frame.

To one side, and somewhat on show, stands Honington's sole example of 'black and white' architecture in the form of the impressively timbered and aptly named Magpie House. Alongside, the approach to the church is a deeply shaded lane bounded either side by high stone walls and towering limes. Ahead, spied through a dark gateway, stands All Saints, its 13th-century tower bathed in sunlight; suddenly, you notice that the air here is not simply clean or sweet – it is positively fragrant.

Once an estate village the houses are no longer 'tied' accommodation for agricultural labourers, but are, today, predominantly privately owned by businesspeople or the retired. Tucked between two cottages, one of which may have been a gatehouse, an extravagantly baroque gateway bars entry to the immediate grounds of Honington Hall. This was Sir Henry Parker's fine red brick mansion, built by him in the late 17th century on the site of an earlier Elizabethan property to which would have belonged the stables and dovecote with its wonderful revolving ladder.

The local milkman can deliver eggs, bacon, bread, fruit juice and potatoes, but after breakfast villagers must travel the 1.5km (1 mile) or so to Shipston on Stour for their shopping. They must go further – to Stratford itself – for entertainment, although living in such a wonderfully peaceful little village must be ample compensation.

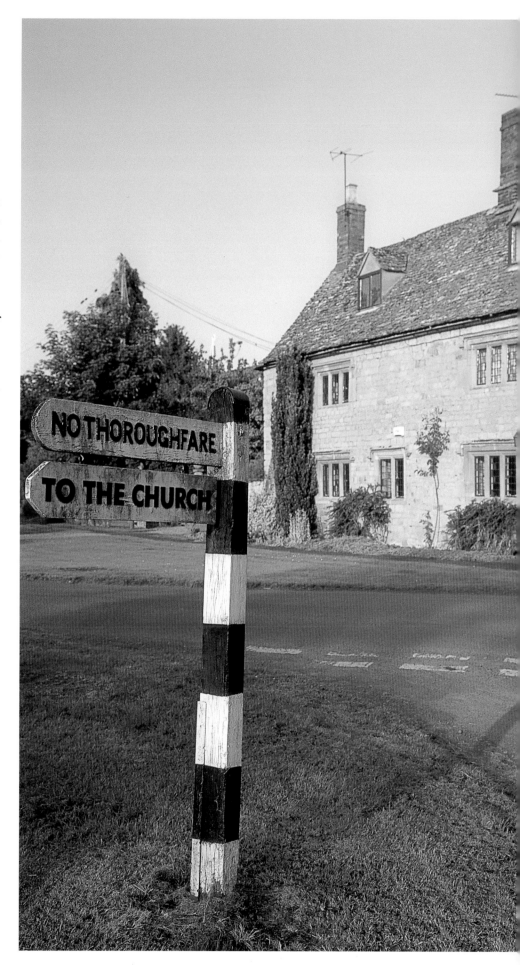

# WELFORD ON AVON

## WARWICKSHIRE

Caught in a kink of the River Avon, the village of Welford lies 6.5km (4 miles) south-west of Stratford-upon-Avon at the end of the Vale of Evesham. It is an interesting mixture of 17th-century thatched cottages and 20th-century 'executive' housing, connected by a haphazard collection of miscellaneous Victorian residences and can boast a pair of old village centres that have as their focal points two very different greens. This gives it something of a split personality, yet both sides are worth getting to know.

At the northern end of the village, the Maypole Green is the social hub of the community. Here villagers gather around the base of what is thought to be one of the largest permanent maypoles in England; and not just for maypole and morris dancing, but for other social events as well, such as the summer fair and carol-singing on Christmas Eve. The Shakespeare pub is close by, as are the Maypole Stores, Memorial Hall, butcher's shop and bus shelter, making this one of Welford's busiest areas.

However, the Welford that visitors come to see can be found at the other end of the High Street. Probably the oldest part of the village, Bell Green is where you will find the post office and the Bell inn as well as the very best of Welford's 65 individually listed buildings, including the wonderful Tudor Vale. But the one that gets the most attention is Ten Penny Cottage, which for the past 400 years has sat on the corner of Boat Lane.

*RIGHT: Decked out in red, white and blue stripes, with a weathervane in the shape of a fox at its tip this is one of the largest permanent maypoles in the country.*

Over the centuries it has gradually been surrounded by further excellent examples of thatch and timber framing, all set within picturesque cottage gardens. Seen together with the parish church in the background, they present one of the most quintessentially English of architectural groupings.

Welford's list of rectors goes back to 1065, but St Peter's Church is another of Sir George Gilbert Scott's mid-19th-century remodellings. While some of the church's earlier elements have been retained the roofed lychgate is a modern reproduction and the village stocks and pound have been lost altogether. Yet for all the changes that have taken place in Welford, including the recent expansion of modern housing, you never forget that the open countryside of pasture and meadow is right on your doorstep.

Despite the many street names reflecting Welford's proximity to water, the inhabitants of the village have almost no access to the river by which they are all but surrounded. Unfortunately, the Avon does

occasionally come to them. The Four Alls near the narrow stone bridge is a riverside pub that has required post-flood refurbishment on more than one occasion. Its name refers to a popular saying: 'the king rules for all, the priest prays for all, the soldier fights for all and the citizen pays for all'.

Reflecting Welford's early development as an agricultural community, its cottages were built wherever was most convenient and from whatever materials could be most easily garnered from the immediate surroundings. This dictated the distribution and arrangement of the village's earliest housing and led to the formation of discrete pockets of habitation separated by clear expanses of open ground, all connected by a network of footpaths and lanes. The relatively recent devastation of the village landscape wrought by Dutch elm disease may also be a contributing factor to the feeling of openness so valued by villagers today.

In the past, much of the village was given over to the cultivation of different varieties of cherry, plum and damson, all of which flourished on the rich alluvial soil of the area. Today farming in the area is predominantly arable, with large, regularly shaped fields edged by low hedges and a handful of trees. The census of 1851 showed that the vast majority of villagers worked on the land or in associated trades. Thirty years later, roughly the same pattern persisted, although the number of those attending school had risen considerably due to the Education Act of 1870. These days, most residents commute from the village to reach their senior schools, colleges and employment, leaving mainly retired and business people and a few horticultural workers. Yet there is still a strong sense of community in Welford. With over 30 local societies and a range of annual festivities, there are plenty of activities that provide an opportunity for villagers to come together and collectively let their hair down.

*ABOVE: Welford's much photographed collection of thatched properties grouped attractively around the church includes the well known Ten Penny cottage.*

# ASHBY ST LEDGERS

## NORTHAMPTONSHIRE

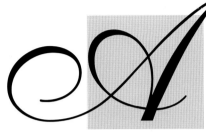

Ashby, derived from the Old Scandinavian 'askrby', is encountered frequently in this part of the country and means 'village where ash trees grow'. But there is an alternative explanation, Aski was once a personal name and so perhaps this was once 'Aski's farmstead'. Known as Ascebi at Domesday the first documented reference to the affix 'St Ledgers' comes in the 13th century when the village was recorded as Esseby Sancti Leodegarii, referring to the dedication of the medieval church of St Leodegarius.

Surrounded by the low Northamptonshire hills, Ashby is a sturdy but attractive estate village of cottages built from amber-coloured ironstone, with stout brick chimneys and roofs of silver-grey Norfolk reed thatch. It does indeed look every inch a farmstead, although the cottages are no longer tied to estate farms. Nowadays, most

are privately owned and their owners commute, for the M1 is only 6.5km (4 miles) distant. Unable to hide their humble origins, and all the more pleasant for it, the buildings of Ashby have been mooted as the prettiest in the county. On the other hand, the village also boasts six thatched farm-workers' cottages with origins that are anything but humble. They were part of a 1908 commission by the architect Edward Lutyens for the estate's then-owner, Viscount Wimborne.

Elsewhere in the village, there are charming examples of true vernacular architecture. The former bakehouse would not only have been a source of bread but also a place where the villagers' Sunday dinners could be cooked in an oven, rather than being boiled in a pot hanging over the fire. A 'country' education was available (with an emphasis on practical matters) in the tiny schoolroom, whose size reflected both the small number of children in the village and the even smaller number expected to attend; their wages being a vital supplement to the meagre income of an agricultural labourer. The post office was run from the home of whichever villager had been selected by the General Post Office and approved by the lord of the manor. There was also, of course, the village forge or smithy. Not much bigger than its furnace, it was a busy place on cold, wet days when things would be slack in the fields; after the alehouse, it was the place where the menfolk would gather in the warmth amid the smoke and the sparks, to put the world (or at least the world they were aware of) to rights.

A large rectangular piece of grass with a bench passes for a village green in Ashby, and at the entrance to the classic old stables of the 'big house' (now converted into apartments), the village pump stands idly by. The latter recalls the days before water was piped into people's houses, first from the lake on the estate and then from the mains supply by the water board. Nearby, a 19th-century farmhouse and its outbuildings have reinvented themselves as a coaching inn, complete with low beams and stabling for the horses while, in a more recent conversion, an old barn has become a fine new village hall with greater accessibility for all and a replacement roof of Polish thatch.

However, the real 'attractions' in the village are both medieval. The Church of the Blessed Virgin Mary and St Leodegarius has a Norman tower and font as well as many old treasures, but it is the paintings on the tower walls that capture the imagination. Among them, a wonderful skeleton is depicted as a sexton, while nearby stands Old Father Time. Next door, the manor gatehouse is not simply important for its architectural features or its great age, but for the part it once played in the history of the country.

In 1605, the manor of Ashby St Ledgers was the home of Lady Catesby, whose son Robert would often entertain a group of 'friends' in the gatehouse. The manor had belonged to the family for two and a half centuries, but the act of treason plotted in its gatehouse and the well known sequence of events that followed meant that Lady Catesby would be the last to live there. There are those who believe it should be an effigy of her son that is placed on top of the bonfire during the traditional November 5th firework celebrations rather than that of the foreign mercenary, Guido Fawkes.

# DUDDINGTON

## NORHAMPTONSHIRE

A village that appears to have been carved from the hill upon which it stands, Duddington is a remarkable union of warm limestone and cool slate. The northern entrance to the village takes you over a weak bridge with origins in the 14th century and alongside a wonderful 17th-century mill, with the River Welland coursing past.

Not that the water always flowed with such vigour, however. Dissatisfied with the performance of his water-driven mill, Nicholas Jackson, the local squire and builder of Duddington's fine manor house, set about identifying the problem. He decided that the river was expending too much energy wandering around its valley in inefficient loops and curves, and that a much straighter course was required to increase its motive capabilities. Consequently, in 1664 he had one cut.

Past the mill, the village sweeps up and around the hill in a broad curve matching the bend in the river, its main street no longer choked with traffic since the opening of two bypasses in the early 1970s. Attractive cottages in the local buff-coloured limestone advance purposefully up the steep incline. Most of their roofs are covered by slates from nearby Collyweston, with the result that the oldest have acquired that slightly saggy quality common to all buildings topped with heavy stone for any length of time. The liberal planting of climbers and the mottling effect of moss and lichen soften the angularity of the thin stone slabs and help to marry the buff walls with the dark grey roofs.

Cottages here range in date from the mid-17th century onwards. Some are humble and crumbling, others sit grandly behind ornamental gates and a long drive. Whether large or small, ancient or modern, the buildings are knitted together by twisting country lanes, long stretches of stone walls and glorious hillside views of the valley below.

Duddington is mentioned in the Domesday Book, but an even earlier Saxon presence was confirmed here in 1994, when the only recorded Anglo-Saxon coin hoard to be found in the area was unearthed by two men building a wall in the village. The linen bagful of 36 silver pennies was probably hidden in the late 9th century AD at around the time the Vikings took control of the region, which was then known as the kingdom of Mercia. Perhaps the money belonged to the man called Dodda who gave his name to the estate: we shall never know.

St Mary's Church is the oldest building in the village. Behind the heavy 13th-century iron-studded door can be found a Norman nave and a 14th-century chancel. Oddly, the two parts of the church are not completely in alignment. It seems that while the earlier builders had followed the previous Saxon orientation of 'true' East the more sophisticated masons of the Middle Ages used magnetic East instead. Yet the most interesting feature of this noble old church has to be the many monuments to generation after generation of the Jackson family.

The village green, now quite small, once extended some considerable distance from the church to the manor house, itself a superb building enlarged several times since Nicholas Jackson's day. It still belongs to the Jackson family, which, considering the indomitable nature of their ancestor, does not come as so much of a surprise as perhaps it should.

*RIGHT:*
*Duddington's impos-*
*ing 17th century*
*stone-built water*
*mill originally*
*owned by the then*
*lord of the manor,*
*Nicholas Jackson was*
*able to harnesses the*
*power of the River*
*Welland more*
*efficiently after its*
*course was straight-*
*ened in 1664.*

# HALLATON

## LEICESTERSHIRE

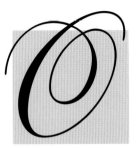

Often described as the 'quintessential English village', Hallaton, set in the valley of the River Welland, is really a decayed market town, which, until the rise of Market Harborough 14.5km (9 miles) to the south-west, could support a weekly market and four annual fairs.

The name of the village means 'farmstead in a nook of land or narrow valley' in Old English, and the surrounding lush grassy slopes were clearly the main attraction for the Saxon settlers who built their wooden village and church here. But there had been a fortification at Castle Hill, just outside Hallaton, more than 1,000 years previously when Iron Age Britons, faced with invaders from Rome, excavated defensive ditches.

In Norman times iron was worked here and to defend this valuable site a motte-and-bailey castle was built about 800m (0.5 mile) to the west of Alctone, as Hallaton was known in 1086. They updated the earlier earthworks with a wooden fortress, and replaced the Saxons' wooden church with one of stone. It has been rebuilt again since, for by the 1200s the village of Hallaton had grown into a prosperous town whose

OPPOSITE: *Signifying the site for a market a butter cross is not always a cruciform – Hallaton's is conical with a small ball finial.*

BELOW: *In the 17th century water was pumped to the Conduit House behind the old smithy and could be collected from there by bucket.*

people were in a position to eschew the local ironstone and import limestone for a magnificent new church, with one of the finest 13th-century towers in the land.

No fewer than five local roads converge here: an indication of Hallaton's former importance in the region. As the settlement expanded, a dense web of streets was woven across the side of the hill, a pattern that has been largely retained to this day. A further sign of prosperity can be found in the village's long rows of houses dating from the 17th to the 19th centuries The oldest are of ironstone with limestone windows, while from 1700 locally produced bricks

began to be used. Small thatched cottages mingle with tall houses of smooth ashlar blocks topped with tile or slate. Walls are rendered, colour-washed or patterned with purple bricks, and fancy chimney pots perch like chess pieces above ornamental thatched roof ridges. Yet the surrounding hills still make their presence felt: passageways punched through buildings to give access to the fields beyond afford glimpses of green countryside. Consequently, Hallaton retains a distinctly rural aspect. But the village's remote location meant that in time it lost out to more accessible markets and its prosperity declined. Today, it displays an enchanting shabby gentility, presenting a somewhat world-weary face that looks a little patched together yet full of character and charm.

This is a wonderfully ancient place where time clearly has not stood still, but has left its mark instead. The old ways still make themselves felt in Hallaton: the small sloping green, with its famous conical butter cross, is the site for the climax of the annual 'bottle-kicking' competition held on Easter Monday. In an age-old ritual, villagers compete with the neighbouring village of Medbourne in a disorderly scrum over three small casks of beer while, not far away, a field behind the thatched Bewick Arms pub is the venue for the ancient 'hare pie scrambling' contest. These festivities hark back to the days of Celtic fertility rites, when the hare was regarded as a sacred creature. It is no coincidence that a Christian shrine, the holy well of St Morrell, was once sited on Hare Pie Hill, or that custom dictates that the parson must provide the pie that is broken up and fought for, since Pagan and Christian traditions so often become inextricably intertwined.

# ALREWAS

## STAFFORDSHIRE

lders growing beside the River Trent gave their name to the Saxon village that developed in their shade. However, the Saxons were not the first people to discover that all they needed was here, for there is evidence of an Iron Age farmstead only 800m (1 mile) distant. Those settlers, too, would have realized that the location offered a plentiful and reliable supply of fresh water, rich alluvial soil perfect for cultivation, and riverside meadows where their beasts could graze. Within easy reach were thick upland forests that could provide kindling for fires and the stout timbers needed for the construction of homes, while the reeds that grew in abundance in the marshes could be used for roofs, floor coverings and baskets.

The area's communications were also good. An old Roman road called Ryckneld Street (later to become part of the A38) passed just to the east, while the busy waterways of the Trent and Tame could be forded not far away. In later years, traders in salt from the north-west created another route, Salter's Way, that went through the village itself. With so many travellers passing through the area, there was ample opportunity for commerce and growth at Alrewas. Nevertheless, fishing and farming remained the mainstays of the local economy. In the early 9th century AD, Bishop Aethelwald of Lichfield cathedral established a prebend at Alrewas, and the Domesday Book records a thriving community with a healthy eel fishery. By 1290, the village had grown so prosperous that Edward I granted it a market charter.

The Middle Ages saw the village develop along the main street and to the north in the vicinity of All Saints Church. It is in these areas that we find the wonderful 'magpie' cottages from the 16th and 17th centuries, with their distinctive square panels and lovely thatched roofs, of which the village is justly proud. Many of the high-quality timber-framed properties in Main Street were farmhouses. Only after enclosure, when the communal 'open' fields that once surrounded the village were parcelled up and distributed in blocks, did the need arise for a farmer to live away from its centre. Today the old marketplace, once so important to the agricultural community, is nothing but a wide road junction, and the 37 farms present in the village in the 1930s have been reduced to a mere handful.

In the 1770s, the first section of what would later be the Trent and Mersey Canal was cut through the north-western edge of the village. Fradley Junction, only 3km |(2 miles) to the south, was eventually to become the hub of the country's inland waterway system. Soon the sides of the cut through Alrewas were lined with wharves and the village began to look away from farming and fishing for the first time in its history.

The Mill Stream, another artificial stretch of water, had originally been excavated to power an ancient flour mill, but at the end of the 18th century a cotton mill was erected on the site. When it later burned down, a replacement was built, although it has since been converted into apartments. Indeed, the impact of modern development has been felt throughout the village, the largest concentration being to the south of Main Street. The old working buildings now house new businesses (one has become a chocolate factory) or, like the old blacksmith's shop, they have been converted for residential use.

*RIGHT: Alrewas (pronounced Awl-russ) is set beside the River Trent. It is a favourite stopping place for narrow boat enthusiasts travelling the Trent and Mersey canal and can boast the largest concentration of timber-framed properties in the county.*

# ACTON BURNELL

## SHROPSHIRE

H idden in a confusion of narrow country lanes, Acton Burnell is such a quiet, unassuming place that to discover a rich vein of history running through it comes as something of a surprise. As with all villages built on a crossroads, some directions prove more rewarding than others, but here one in particular seems to have cornered the market in visual appeal and historical interest. A battered brown sign points you in the direction of 'The Castle' along a broad leafy lane that seems to lead nowhere, except back in time. At its end a wide gate opens onto a wide dirt track along which can be found a trio of ancient relatives.

In the late 13th century, Robert Burnell, from whose family the village gets half of its name, was chaplain to the young Prince Edward. They clearly got along because, following his coronation in 1274, Edward I made Robert his Lord Chancellor; a year later he was also elected Bishop of Bath and Wells. In 1283, the king visited the bishop at his home in Acton Burnell and while there summoned a parliament. It is said to have assembled in a vast tithe barn, 45m (150 feet) in length, forever after known as Parliament Barn. Perhaps this event encouraged Robert to provide a more

OPPOSITE: *The striking red sandstone ruins of Acton Burnell Castle are now in the care of English Heritage.*

BELOW: *Once the Stag & Huntsman, Acton Burnell's only pub has been converted into the Village Store.*

impressive setting for the next royal visit as before long a major building project was underway on land adjacent to Parliament Barn. Tall towers of dramatic red sandstone rose high above the tiny village, though whether or not the king ever saw the greatly improved Burnell residence is not recorded.

Bishop Burnell was also responsible for the construction of the diminutive church of St Mary (although its tower is Victorian), which is now almost hidden by the tall grass of its churchyard and the shadows of the castle walls. By the mid-20th century, this simple medieval church with its small tower was in need of restoration, but raising the necessary finance proved something of a challenge. Finally, the Lee family of Virginia, USA, stepped in. The original Lees of Langley, a small hamlet to the south of Acton Burnell, had succeeded the Burnells as lords of the manor. One of their descendants, Richard Henry Lee, signed the Declaration of Independence while another, General Robert E. Lee, led the forces of the South in the American Civil War, but it seems that the family never forgot its connection with Acton Burnell.

After the castle, barn and church, the rest of the village can seem something of an anticlimax, but it is not without interest, although satellite dishes do detract a little from its overall appeal. The village school closed in 1988, but there remain some lovely timber-framed houses in black and white and others of an attractive grey stone while Acton Burnell Hall, a fine Georgian mansion, rebuilt in 1914 following a devastating fire, is now a college. No longer the haunt of royalty or the exalted, today the pretty village of Acton Burnell seems perfectly comfortable with its relative obscurity.

# CLAVERLEY

## SHROPSHIRE

Built on a slope, Claverley is always either uphill or downhill, yet for all its vaguely unsettling 'wonkiness' it still has one of the most captivating of all village centres. An immediate impact is made by the striking 15th-century (and possibly partly 13th-century) timber-framed vicarage, its black-and-white walls a dazzling display of close studwork decorated with chevrons and short diagonals. The wide leaded-light windows of its gabled end look out over a narrow path into the churchyard, reached by way of a substantial black-and-white lychgate, or not as the mood or direction of approach takes you now that some railings have been removed. Before you, amid the weathered stones and crumbling tombs of villagers past, rises the imposing red sandstone tower of gothic All Saints Church. But no matter how impressive the decorative exterior may appear, inside it is even more wonderful.

There are not one but two ancient fonts. The first is a massive stone bowl dating from early Saxon times, which may indicate the presence of a substantial church here towards the end of the 7th century AD. The other, possibly Saxon, or perhaps Norman, probably belonged to the third church to stand on this site, some of the fabric of which can still be seen in the present structure and whose construction is credited to Leofric, Earl of Mercia and husband of Lady Godiva.

Much of the rest of the church is Norman, including the superb frieze above the arcade on the north side of the nave. Painted in around the year 1200, it is probably not, as some have thought, a skirmish from the Battle of Hastings, but is more likely to illustrate the Psychomachia, a 4th-century allegorical poem by the Roman Prudentius concerning the struggle between the seven Christian virtues and the seven pagan vices – a popular subject at that time. But these are by no means the only wall paintings in this surprising old church. When the colours were still bright and the details crisp, the overall impact of such rich imagery on the humble worshippers standing beneath must have been truly awe-inspiring.

Claverley's remarkable church serves as an evocative reminder of the central role such places played in the daily lives of the early villagers. It is easy to forget that long ago churches were far more than just places of worship: they were truly the heart of community life providing a place of refuge in times of danger, and, in more settled times, a meeting place similar to today's village hall (in those days there were no cumbersome pews to get in the way). Important announcements would be nailed to the church door for the few who could read, but word would soon spread, while the walls inside could impart pictorial enlightenment.

Later, the village alehouse took on many of these roles. Not far from the church, two present-day pubs, the Kings Arms and the Crown, maintain the black-and-white theme carried on through many of the village's attractive, creeper-clad cottages. Claverley is an exceedingly charming village with lots of delightful little details. Outside the post office is a late Georgian pump, its stone trough planted with flowers, while above it have been fixed three signs that read 'High Street', 'Claverley' and 'Telegraph Office'. Only one is of much use, assuming you know in which village you happen to be standing.

*OPPOSITE: A black-and-white lychgate leads from an area called the Bull Ring (possibly where the animals were once baited) alongside the market cross, and past the Old Vicarage to the splendid sandstone church of All Saints.*

# GREAT BUDWORTH

## CHESHIRE

The tall chimneys of Tudor England are much in evidence in this highly decorative village. Black and white, brick and timber or just plain brick – though actually never plain – these story-book houses manage to climb a steep slope and span the long centuries from Shakespeare to Victoria at one and the same time.

This 'enclosure of a man named Budda' was sited on a green hill above lush grassy meadows and wide glassy meres. Later known as Budewrde, although not yet 'great', the settlement was still worthy of a mention in William's post-Conquest long list of lists. There is no Little Budworth, so its 'greatness' must derive from its former position at the centre of the largest parish in Cheshire that at one time contained no fewer than 35 townships.

Here, sturdy oak timbers that have become silver-grey with age support uneven walls organic in their asymmetry. A row of black-and-white cottages, 'keeping their feet dry' by perching atop low walls of red sandstone blocks, almost look newly built behind a chain of archways formed by carefully lopped trees. Others sit sedately upon courses of red brick. There is ornamentation everywhere: a frieze painted in black onto a white plaster band beneath the eaves; countless examples of imaginatively patterned brickwork; wonderful little details on a gabled end or around a mullioned window. There is a richness of texture here and what appears to be a mania for climbing plants, with festoons of wisteria or Russian vine that make the houses disappear back into the wooded hillside.

The George and Dragon, built in 1722 (with a new front added in 1875) is practically smothered in Virginia creeper. Several windows have already been covered and it looks like the doorway will be the next to go, yet the pub appears altogether different in the winter months when bare spidery tendrils weave webs across the white and red brick facade. Outside is a fence upon which has been carved mottoes such as 'God speed the plough' and 'Beware ye Beelzebub', while over the doorway of the pub can be seen a verse warning against intemper-

OPPOSITE: *Ornamentation and adornment abound in this surprising little village, restored from near dereliction by the Victorian Squire Warburton.*

BELOW: *Great Budworth's tiny sub-post office is one of the most attractive and unusual of its kind in the country.*

ance, penned by the 19th-century poet and squire of Great Budworth, Rowland Eyes Egerton-Warburton. Sir John Warburton had been a knight in Elizabeth I's reign, and the family has its own chapel in the church. Four hundred years later, his poetically inclined descendant is credited with having saved Great Budworth from dereliction and earns praise for having done so without 'destroying its unique character'. Squire Warburton held very strong opinions on the subject of restoration and much that we see in the village today is a result of the work over which he presided.

Visitors to Great Budworth will admire Sir John Dean's superb Jacobean schoolhouse in the churchyard, as well as the 14th-century crenellations and carving that bedeck the church itself, but few realize that the village has another treasure. A quaint little building with wrought iron gates stands at the foot of the hill on the old coach road to London. Commissioned by Squire Warburton from leading Liverpool architect Edmund Kirby in 1869, it contains the 'Running Pump' by which spring water was piped from a brick chamber in the Dene wood nearby. From as long ago as the 17th century, this had been the village's only supply of fresh water, until five new pumps were installed around the settlement in 1890. Even after the arrival of mains water in 1936, the untreated variety available at the Running Pump was still preferred by many.

Great Budworth today is virtually a dormitory village, with high property prices and only a few workng farms remaining in the area, but it remains very much an imaginative 19-century squire's vision of how an English village should be.

# LYMM

## CHESHIRE

*BELOW: Having passed through a patch of woodland called The Dingle, the Dane is held back by Lymm's lower dam.*

**N**umerous natural springs flow through the sandstone rocks upon which this village is built. In fact, Lymm – or Lime as the Domesday Book would have it – means 'the noisy stream or torrent'. Today, however, most of the water in and around the village (and there is plenty of it) is notably quiet and placid.

Artefacts discovered in the area have led some to theorize that Lymm may once have been a place of worship for the Romans; it has even been suggested that the worn sandstone steps on which the village's centuries-old cross stands could have formed part of a shrine to the goddess Minerva. Temple-like, with four columns supporting a heavy stone roof that sports both a simple sundial and an ornate weathervane, the cross itself has been dated to anywhere between the 14th and 17th centuries. Whatever its true age, it has been a landmark and gathering place in Lymm for countless generations. In earlier times, the villagers no doubt came to witness the spectacle at the stocks, but now they assemble there for purely social reasons.

A promising Saxon settlement in the 7th century AD, by the end of the 1400s Lymm's farmsteads had flourished into a prosperous agricultural community. Yet only 100 years later a change of direction had taken place and a good deal of industrial development was underway. An increase in quarrying was followed by the expansion of other industries such as tanning and iron working.

Construction of the Bridgewater Canal began in 1759, the cut going right through the centre of Lymm. What the locals made of this is unknown but as they had no say in the matter the new waterway seems to have been quickly accepted as part of the daily life of the village. Originally built to facilitate the transportation of coal, the canal greatly improved communications and served to encourage further industrial growth. Mills were built, as well as new cottages for the expanding workforce and larger houses for the managers and owners. Many of the older properties in the village are simply constructed from blocks carved from the local red sandstone, while the later and more prestigious dwellings are of brick.

Lymm Dam was constructed in the early 19th century in an attempt to meet the ever-growing demand for power. It meant re-routing the turnpike road and creating a series of reservoirs and waterfalls along the course of a stream called the Dane. Then, in 1853, the London and North Western Railway finally reached the settlement, heralding a new phase of expansion and rebuilding.

Finally, as the century drew to a close, the Manchester Ship Canal was cut just to the north of the village. Even so, and despite its best efforts, without a local supply of coal Lymm's industries became uncompetitive. By 1989 the rail line was closed and the canal had become a leisure amenity; today the once-busy towpath is a very pleasant place for a stroll.

The Lymm we see now is largely a pleasant mixture of the very old and the very Victorian, although being located only 22km (14 miles) from the centre of Manchester, means that the village has inevitably expanded rapidly in recent years. Even so, the modern development

blends successfully with the old, assisted by an abundance of mature trees and clever planting that ensures the village retains a vestige of rural character. It still has a traditional market every Thursday as well as a good selection of shops, and uses every advantage it possesses, both man-made and naturally given, to the maximum effect.

One day people may visit Lymm to wonder at the mysterious complex of caves there, when investigations into its nature and significance have been concluded. Archaeologists are only now beginning to unravel the mystery of Lymm's past, but in the present it remains a handsome village that never quite made the transition to industrial town, and is all the better for it.

*ABOVE: Lymm's enigmatic market cross may be the only one in the country with its own dedicated web cam.*

# CROMFORD

## DERBYSHIRE

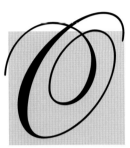

Once called simply 'the ford by the river bend', the Crunforde mentioned in the Domesday Book has more recently become known as 'Richard Arkwright's Village'. Celebrated as the birthplace of the factory system its part in the story of the Industrial Revolution is so well known that Cromford seems content to let visitors assume that before the former Bolton wig-maker arrived with his ingenious new spinning frame, there was nothing here at all. Yet in 1771, England's first water-powered cotton mill was built close to a medieval bridge, one of the oldest in Derbyshire, that had carried the ancient community of yeoman farmers and lead miners at Cromford across the fast-flowing waters of the River Derwent since the 15th century.

Climbing a steep slope between limestone cliffs and outcrops of dark millstone grit, the scattered hamlet of Cromford had once been part of Edward the Confessor's royal manor of Wirksworth. Before Arkwright's arrival, its economy was based on sheep farming, with a few cultivated fields of wheat, barley and oats, and lead mining, centred on an area of the village known as the Scarthin. Yet by the mid-17th century, the industrial sector was experiencing problems, with flooding in the mines. Drainage tunnels (soughs) were constructed, but although they solved the immediate problem, the industry failed to thrive as formerly.

It was the opening in 1771 of a paper mill just outside nearby Matlock Bath, successfully harnessing the power of the River Derwent that proved to be the turning point for Cromford. Not only did it provide employment for the struggling lead workers, it also pointed the way to a new, cheap source of power for Richard Arkwright's revolutionary cotton-spinning machines. Using stone from the demolished Steeple Hall at Wirksworth, the fortress-like Cromford Mill was constructed. Five storeys high (later sections reached seven storeys), its forbidding appearance probably owes as much to Arkwright's fear of machine wreckers, and militant spinners as it does to practicality and economy.

Power for the machinery was controlled by damming the Bonsall Brook that ran down through the village to the mill, creating a series of reservoirs along its course, and also by diverting water drained from the lead workings by the Cromford Sough. As for manpower, the workforce drawn from the existing population was soon supplemented by families from much further afield. To accommodate them, Arkwright financed some of the earliest purpose-built

LEFT: *Houses and shops lining the Scarthin Promenade overlook Cromford Pond, a reservoir created for the mill.*

BELOW: *A mid-19th-century overshot water-wheel once used to grind locally mined minerals used in the production of paint.*

industrial housing in the country: three-storeyed terraces of the local gritstone. Dark, simple and unadorned, they had wide windows on the upper floors to light workshops that contained framework looms. Here, outworkers could complete the textile manufacturing process by weaving the product from the mill into cloth.

In less than a generation, the tiny village was transformed. It had gained a school, two chapels, a Sunday school, shops and a fine hotel for the mill owner's business associates and guests (although the large clock on the front was probably more for the benefit of his millworkers). A charter for a Saturday market at the front of the Greyhound Hotel was granted in 1790, while communications were improved by the construction of a canal complete with wharves and storage buildings. However, before long bigger and better mills were opened elsewhere, some of them built by Arkwright himself, while the mill at Cromford, which had once operated 24 hours a day and employed 200 people, stopped producing cotton in the mid-19th century. The market closed in 1880, although the canal managed to limp on until 1944.

By the end of 1924 the Arkwright family had sold all of their properties in the village, enabling many tenants to purchase their homes. Today, there is much new housing and the village has been separated from the old mill by the busy A6, leading to complaints about noise and pollution within the heart of Cromford itself. The Arkwright Trust is slowly restoring the historic mill after decades of neglect, while the canal has become a popular leisure amenity. The many people who come to Cromford to pay homage or just out of curiosity remain spellbound by every darkened stone and curious alleyway.

# EDENSOR

## DERBYSHIRE

The original village of Edensor (pronounced Ensor) was so named because it had been founded on a 'sloping bank' belonging to a man named Eadin. Although the name remains applicable, for Edensor is still on a slope, it is no longer the same part of the slope occupied by the Edensoure mentioned in the Domesday Book. Today's village is an entirely 19th-century creation dreamt up by a head gardener and a Derby architect, on the instructions of a duke.

In the 18th century, the fourth Duke of Devonshire undertook an immensely costly programme of works to update his seat at Chatsworth. The house was altered and the park re-landscaped, but there remained the problem of a straggling old village on the estate, which, although distant, spoiled the view. There was only one thing for it – the village had to go. Edensor's inhabitants were rehoused in other villages on the estate, such as Pilsley and Beeley, and all cottages visible from the house were removed. This dismantling process was completed some years later by the sixth Duke, who then asked his head gardener, Joseph Paxton, to build another Edensor, only this time somewhere less obtrusive. John Robertson, an up-and-coming architect from Derby, was employed to provide the designs for the cottages, while Paxton was to arrange the siting and layout.

There has been much speculation over what happened next: perhaps the duke was too busy to take a proper look at the drawings Roberson brought him and simply chose at random, or perhaps the young architect was just flexing his 'architectural' muscles. Whatever the reason, between 1838 and 1842 the estate workers' humble cottages were reborn as picturesque villas in a mixed medley of styles incorporating such diverse features as Tudor chimneys and Italianate windows, Jacobean gables and Swiss-chalet roofs, Georgian doorways and medieval castellation. Hardly any edge is left undecorated: gable ends ripple with waves and wooden icicles drip from the eaves, every detail picked out in a single shade: Chatsworth blue. Perhaps if the houses had been built closer together the different elements would jar, but the result is an attractive, if rather odd, village designed for its aesthetic appeal as much as practicality. Yet the villagers were not completely forgotten. Each property had a large garden with plenty of room for both ornamental flowers and useful vegetable plots, while the houses themselves were of a good size.

Intended as accommodation for the officials of the Chatsworth estate, all the properties in the village were tied houses and remain so today. There is now a combined post office, village store and tea rooms occupying one of the original Edensor farmhouses, and the old stable block and coach house have been converted into accommodation for retired estate workers. By virtue of the fact that they had been on the 'right' side of the road and therefore invisible from the stately home, other original buildings also survived. The school, the alehouse, two cottages, a farmhouse and the 14th-century church remained, as did part of the old rectory. However, in 1867 the old church was rebuilt by Sir George Gilbert Scott. Later, in 1948, the school was demolished and now a spacious green planted with laburnum trees sweeps away down the hill before the church.

*RIGHT: When the village of Edensor was re-located out of sight of Chatsworth house the new dwellings were roomy villas for the professional estate employees; all built of the local stone but in an assortment of diverse styles.*

# BERKSWELL

## WEST MIDLANDS

*D*eep in the ancient forest of Arden, the village of Berkswell can boast many of the constituent parts of the quintessential English village. Yet, Berkswell feels fragmented, with few typically English juxtapositions or groupings, just a lot of lovely separate components. Of course, such a concept would have been totally lost on the Angles who named their new home after their leader Bercul. His well was not of the bucket-on-a-rope variety, but a 'wella', or bubbling spring and by the time it came into his possession, it had probably attained some pagan spiritual significance. This particular 'wella' can still be found bubbling, rather sluggishly it must be said, into a stone tank that holds only a shallow pool of algae-rich water before it drains away to the River Blythe.

It was common for early Christians to build churches on or near sites of pagan worship, often obliterating them completely or at the very least assigning to them new meanings. Wells, however, were too useful to do away with altogether, so instead they would be rehabilitated as places of Christian baptism, and what better demonstration than the baptism of a chieftan of Bercul's stature by the monks of Lichfield. Appropriately, the nearby church is dedicated to St John the Baptist. Underneath, a double Norman crypt contains traces of an earlier Saxon stone structure, perhaps from

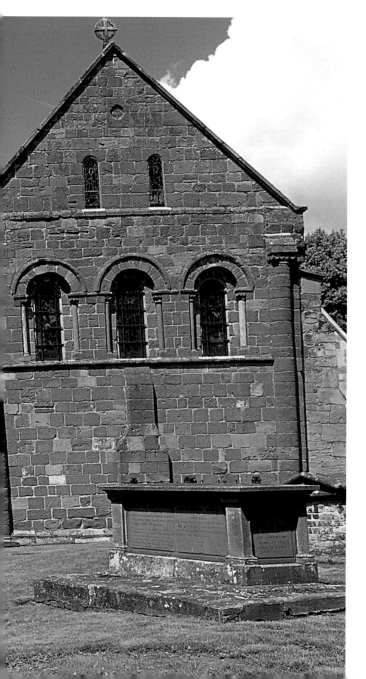

a church founded by Bercul himself. There is evidence that pilgrims may once have visited holy relics in a shrine there, but what makes this church special is the superb half-timbered vestry above the porch. Once the tiny village school, it has been in use since the early 17th century.

Berkswell's present-day school, is only a short walk from the churchyard gate and stands close to a tiny half-timbered house from about 1500, now the village museum, still splendid despite having exchanged thatch for tiles. Opposite, the Well House, a former rectory dating from the 17th century, was the childhood home of Maud Watson, the first Wimbledon Ladies' Champion in 1884, while a minute's walk away, the combined village shop, post office and tea room stands quaintly bow-fronted beside the triangular green, where the five-holed stocks have been puzzling locals and visitors alike for as long as anyone can remember. Tales of a one-legged elderly miscreant are probably apocryphal: it is more likely that the sixth hole has simply been lost to the elements.

Some distance from the green, stands the large Bear and Ragged Staff inn, its name a reference to the emblem of the Earls of Warwick, lords of the manor here in the Middle Ages. The inn was once the venue for the annual hiring fair known as the 'stattis' (statutes) fair, held every October. Each man would display somewhere about his person a sign of his calling – for example, wool for a shepherd or horsehair for a wagoner – the farmers would then select the men who were to work for them during the next 12 months.

In all living communities things must move on and new uses be found for old if they are to survive. Most of Berkswell's farmhouses are, today, simply houses and many modern residences have been built in the wide-open spaces between them. Berkswell Manor is converted into apartments, while historic 16th-century Nailcote Hall has become a hotel, golf and country club. But the past also has a place and recently an old windmill in the village has been restored to full working order.

*LEFT: Opposite a handsome former rectory with decorative Dutch gables, the magnificently carved sandstone Church of St John the Baptist carries both a clock and a sundial on its tower, above a most unusual half-timbered porch.*

# EDWINSTOWE

## NOTTINGHAMSHIRE

*E*dwinstowe is a big and busy village. It was pretty once and is attractive now, but perhaps its best feature is its setting. Once deep in the heart of Sherwood Forest, Edwinstowe now lies at the edge of the best fragments that remain.

A Saxon settlement in a forest clearing, Edwinstowe was the 'holy place of St Eadwine' and has its entry in the Domesday Book. The first church here is likely to have been built of stout Sherwood oak on the very spot where St Edwin, king of Northumbria, was buried after the Battle of Heathfield. Later, in penance for the murder of Thomas à Becket, Henry I rebuilt the church in stone. He also constructed a fine hunting lodge in the adjoining village of Clipstone, which was much frequented by subsequent monarchs, for by now patches of heath and expanses of wood pasture had been opened up in the forest, making it ideal for falconry and the pursuit of deer. In fact, the word 'forest' is a legal term describing an area where special laws were in force to protect its timber and to preserve game for royal hunting parties.

A two-day annual fair was granted to Edwinstowe in the time of Henry IV, which must have caused a stir, albeit briefly, every year. Generally, though, it seems that life

in the village has been peculiarly uneventful over the years. Of course, the villagers would have been aware of the activities of the visiting royals nearby, but perhaps a place where nothing much ever happened was the perfect setting for a legendary hero. Edwinstowe is Robin Hood's village and his statue stands before the local library, holding the hand of the maid he is said to have married in St Mary's Church.

Royal power over the forest declined after the English Civil Wars, and eventually much of the area was divided up between several private landowners. But life for the woodsmen of Edwinstowe remained as uneventful as ever until the 'black gold' of Nottinghamshire was discovered in the late 19th century. The village and many others nearby were found to be sitting on top of a vast seam of coal. Later, Cecil Day-Lewis was to write that during his father's period of service as vicar of St Mary's, which began in

1918, the place had changed from being a 'country village' to a 'mining town'.

Until the nationalization of the coal industry in 1947, local landowners grew wealthy by exploiting this valuable commodity beneath their estates. The fabric of the village reflects not only their good fortune, but also the considerably harsher lives of the many miners and their families brought into the area to work the reserves of Thoresby colliery.

Regeneration is currently underway in Sherwood Forest: new trees are being planted and the great scars left by the mines are being re-landscaped. With conditions much improved, Thoresby colliery remains productive. It is still a place where nothing much out of the ordinary happens, but today we need places like this more than ever. Edwinstowe may well be the quintessential English village of the future – an object lesson in changing with the times yet remaining a true village at heart.

*ABOVE: A pair of trim red-brick cottages whose plain and practical architecture is typical of this working mining village.*

*LEFT: Robin Hood bends his knee and takes the hand of Maid Marian, in front of Edwinstowe's Public Library.*

# The Northern Counties

Villages set against a background of the self-same stone from which they were fashioned so that they subtly merge with their surroundings, and which have a certain uniformity in materials and architectural style, may not instantly delight the eye of one raised on a diet of crooked cottages and softly curving roofs of thatch. For in the uplands of northern England, the vertical and the perpendicular prevail (although the hard edges are not always as plumb as they may at first appear).

The glittering cascades of countless fast-flowing streams, whose power was once harnessed for the mills of early industry, serve only to increase the vertiginous effect.

Yet it is not all rugged rocks and ragged breath. The vales and dales present an altogether gentler proposition (albeit generally a more crowded one) delicately veined with mile upon mile of drystone walls that not only enclose the lush green fields, but connect the lowlands with the wilder reaches above. Nor should we forget the region's isolated villages concealed amidst bleakly attractive moors, or its coastal villages tumbling down spectacular sea cliffs. Those unfamiliar with this part of the country sometimes cling to the mistaken belief that all of its settlements are an austere, monochromatic grey. But what could be warmer than the rich chocolate-brown stone of Lancashire or more vibrant than roof upon roof of intense terracotta pantiles set against the golden sandstone of North Yorkshire?

LEFT: Beautiful Grasmere lake is barely one mile from the village that bears its name. A feature common to all the settlements in this region, from the North West's early industrial centres to the North East's early centres of Christianity and art, is that they are surrounded by spectacular scenery on a grand scale.

# HEPTONSTALL

## WEST YORKSHIRE

*H*eptonstall has been described as 'Haworth without the Brontës'; an observation no doubt intended as a compliment, yet it denies this ancient Pennine village its own very special individual identity. Even less convincing is the epithet of 'Yorkshire's best-kept secret', for it has been said so many times of Heptonstall that one could be forgiven for pointing out that, by now, the cat is most definitely out of the bag.

Nevertheless, enthusiasm for this remarkably well preserved textile village from the pre-factory era is immediately understandable when you venture along its steep, cobbled streets and explore its crooked alleys. The prospect must have been far less enticing to the Viking farmers who arrived 1,500 years ago. They were faced with scratching a precarious living from the desolate hillside, their simple houses squeezed onto narrow ledges or clinging to the precipitous slope high above the Calder Valley. Space has always been at a premium here and so the rugged, dark stone cottages are tightly packed, yet they cluster around the surprising extravagance of a churchyard containing two churches!

*BELOW: Steep cobbled streets and alleys worn smooth by the feet of countless villagers wind between dark stone houses.*

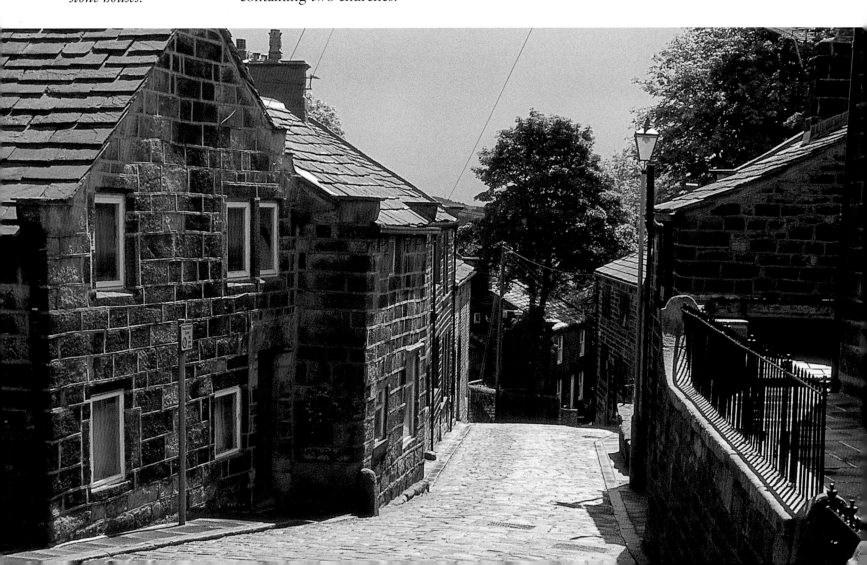

Although Heptonstall means 'farmstead where rosehips or brambles grow', this is no rural idyll. For while its situation is undeniably beautiful, the weather can be cruelly harsh – at times violently so. The 15th-century church of St Thomas à Becket was partly demolished by the great storm of 1847 despite being built low as a precaution, and the mock '15th-century' replacement of St Thomas the Apostle raised alongside it in 1854 was itself badly damaged by lightning 21 years later. Nor does the lack of space only impact upon the living; it is possible that upwards of 10,000 people are buried beneath the tightly packed headstones in Heptonstall's graveyard.

It might be said that this small village has seen far more of death than perhaps it should. Only 12 years after plague had decimated the local population in 1631, Royalist troops attacked a Roundhead garrison at Heptonstall and in the ensuing skirmish suffered heavy losses. Many that did not die fighting were either hit by massive boulders that the Roundheads set rolling down the slope or were drowned in the swollen River Calder below as they tried to retreat.

Even in peacetime life here could be brutal and short. Under such conditions, faith played an important part in the lives of the villagers and in addition to its two Anglican churches, Heptonstall has a third place of worship worthy of mention. In 1764 John Wesley himself laid the foundation stone for Heptonstall's unusual octagonal Methodist church which claims to be the oldest in the world to have remained in continual use.

In pre-industrial times, Heptonstall was a centre for handloom weaving, producing corduroy and worsted, but in the end, the development of water- and steam-powered looms forced the weavers down from the hillside and into the valley, where the village of Hebden Bridge developed rapidly. Heptonstall residents who could not find work in the new mills either turned their hand to farming or were forced into the workhouse, and for a time the village was all but deserted. This exodus, combined with the village's continued inaccessibility, has meant that the

settlement has remained virtually frozen in time at this point in its history.

Towngate, Heptonstall's main street, has hardly changed since the weavers left 200 years ago. Many of the fine old buildings that reflect Heptonstall's former prosperity can still be seen, and the old cloth hall, where the weavers' work was stored survives. There are still few shops or places of public entertainment, although the old grammar school is now Heptonstall Museum. Of the many pubs and alehouses that were once the haunt of the infamous local gangs of 'coiners', only two remain. Most of the present-day villagers travel to Hebden Bridge or even further afield for work.

*ABOVE: Many of the gravestones in Heptonstall's churchyard have been used twice, but as they are often laid flat on the ground, only one of the inscriptions may be seen.*

# ROBIN HOOD'S BAY
## NORTH YORKSHIRE

*I*t is often visited by strangers attracted by the fame of the alum works in its neighbourhood, and the peculiarity of its grotesque appearance'. Such was the verdict of an early 19th-century tourist guide. At that time, Robin Hood's Bay was somewhat different in appearance from the picturesque tangle of narrow cobbled passageways and steep steps that we know today. A later guide described its houses as being 'perched, like the nests of seagulls, among the cliffs', and added that the connections between the streets in some areas were by way of 'a plank bridge thrown over a gully'. Nevertheless, the neatness of the dwellings impressed the writer, who remarked that it could be attributed to a seafaring people's firm grasp of 'the true principles of the economy of space' and long before communications were improved by the arrival of the Scarborough and Whitby railway in 1885, visitors were already making a contribution to the economy of this isolated fishing village.

In 1780, part of King Street, the main road into Robin Hood's Bay, had fallen into the sea together with two rows of cottages, some of which had long been dangerously undercut by the waves. To some contemporary eyes, this calamity greatly improved

*BELOW: Stone cottages, many topped with colourful red pantile roofs are packed tightly together up the sides of a ravine.*

the appearance of the place, although it is doubtful if the owners were as impressed. A few years later, part of Park Road disappeared in a similar fashion, and in 1834 the Bay Hotel slid into the bay. Here the soft limestone cliff recedes at the rate of 7.5cm (3 inches) a year, but it was not until 1975 that Robin Hood's Bay acquired a sea wall. Measuring 12m (40 feet) high and 150m (500 feet) long, it is the highest in Britain.

Many centuries ago, Viking fisher-farmers settled in this narrow ravine. Later, in 1538, the village was described as a 'fisher townlet of twenty boats'. This entry in John Leland's *Itinerary* is the first time we see the name Robin Hood's Bay although any connection with the legendary folk hero is a tenuous one at best. Known locally as Baytown, the village had strong connections with the nearby inland settlement of Raw, so perhaps its name has more to do with the unfamiliarity of the local dialect to the ears of Henry VIII's topographer than with any one individual.

Poor land communications present no obstacle to a seafaring community, and coastal trade flourished to the extent that Robin Hood's Bay overtook both Scarborough and Whitby in terms of importance. At the same time, the villagers took part in a lucrative but strictly illegal sideline. Highly taxed items such as tea, playing cards, spinning wheels and chocolate would be loaded into fishing boats from continental ships waiting just offshore and then smuggled into the village.

By the beginning of the 19th century, the fishing fleet had grown to 35 cobles (small open-topped fishing boats) and 5 large herring boats, manned by around 130 fishermen. It was an industry that involved almost the entire community: the womenfolk salted the fish and packed them into barrels, or baited the lines, while the children would make lobster pots or mend nets; but by the end of the century, the fishing industry was in serious decline. The small harbour could not accommodate large offshore trawlers of the kind that began operating out of Whitby, and by the outbreak of the First World War only two fishing families were left in the village. In recent years, how-

ever, Robin Hood's Bay has become known as one of the best crab-fishing grounds in the north and the industry has seen a modest revival.

Robin Hood's Bay is now one of the most picturesque and best known villages along the North Yorkshire coast. Its famous tumble of red pantile roofs and the fossil-rich 'scars' that shine darkly in the bay at low tide attract many thousands of visitors every year. These days, cars are strongly discouraged from making the steep descent into the village – a sensible precaution because the narrow streets are usually full of people admiring the view.

*ABOVE: Fossil hunters take advantage of low tide in the bay when a large area of the seabed is exposed.*

# THORNTON LE DALE
## NORTH YORKSHIRE

Thornton le Dale, Thornton Dale or just plain Thornton, this pleasant village will answer to all three. There is always something vaguely disconcerting about buying a picture postcard of the 'picture postcard' village in which you stand. On many occasions, the photograph on the card is so out of date that it bears little resemblance to the place it purports to depict, but this is unlikely to be a problem in Thornton: although its name may change, the village itself never seems to alter.

Thornton is widely held to be one of the prettiest villages in the North Riding. The discerning tourists of the '20s and '30s thought so too, and in the intervening decades it would seem that only the shapes and makes of the cars have changed. Located right on the edge of the North Yorkshire moors, the village is appealing and trim, with its less attractive features very properly camouflaged or tucked away out of sight. The large but necessary car park is invisible behind trees and tea rooms, and the modern development is generally hidden by older and more picturesque buildings of pleasantly worn limestone. Unfortunately, there is not much to be done about the few short stretches of urban development that disfigure the A170 in places, except perhaps to discourage people from travelling by that route.

*RIGHT: Access to the Post Office is gained via one of the many small bridges across the Thornton Beck.*

*BELOW LEFT: Colourful gardens crowd the bank between beck and cottage wall making this one of the most photographed parts of the village.*

*BELOW: Lovely stone cottages line the beck and are reached from the street by simple stone or wooden bridges.*

A small green sits in one of the right angles of the central crossroads, its ancient market cross and not-so-ancient stocks resting in dappled leafy shade, while the opposing corners are filled with attractive shops. Further along in the direction of Scarborough is the long, low row of Lady Lumley's 17th-century almshouses, completed in 1670. They terminate at the corner with the grammar school, founded a decade or so earlier and endowed by the same lady, who as owner of the Thornton estate lived at the hall.

Church and hall remain very much behind the scenes. The latter is now a care home for the elderly, its Tudor beginnings masked by an 18th-century facade. Meanwhile, All Saints Church, perched upon a hill, was rebuilt in the 14th century but retains its 12th-century font. By contrast, the superb Methodist church prefers to be in the thick of things and sits squeezed in between lanes and houses opposite the post office. Bride, groom, bridesmaids and guests cheerfully block the narrow pavement as traffic stops to allow photographs to be taken from the other side of the street.

Clearly the star of the show, Thornton Beck barrels down from the hills sweeping past a much-photographed thatched cottage and on under the bridge carrying the A170. However, by the time it has completed its grand arabesque through the centre of the village, it has been divided and pacified. Thereafter it is content to run prettily along the side of the road to Malton, before darting out of sight beneath the tarmac. The lovely stone cottages along its length, with their attractive little bridges and colourful gardens, are perhaps the sight that most people remember whenever Thornton is mentioned.

# WARTER

## EAST YORKSHIRE

*arter is an extraordinarily shabby village, but the population is far from being wretched. They have to put up with mossy, mouldy thatch, with bulging walls, uneven floors, windows that will not open and doors that will not shut. They have to sleep in windowless, chimneyless lofts; but even the worst of these hovels is highly valued, and highly paid for'.* Inquiry on the State of the Dwellings of Rural Labourers, Dr H. J. Hunter, 1865.

Today, Warter is considered one of the prettiest villages in the Yorkshire Wolds, but its much-photographed cottages represent a comparatively recent improvement of a long-standing situation. Dr Hunter made his report more than a century after a Warter estate steward had been moved to comment on the sorry state of houses there. The gradual rebuilding of Warter had clearly been proceeding slowly since the Penington family bought up nearly all the freehold land in the late 18th century thus turning it into a 'closed' village. When they owned everything, except for the church, the Peningtons proceeded to demolish one-third of the houses.

It was common practice in 'closed' villages to keep the amount of housing on the estate to an absolute minimum. If labourers were forced to live outside the village, the poor rates (levied locally to support the community's sick and unemployed) were guaranteed to be low. Consequently, the lord of the manor could charge tenant farmers, often the main contributors to such taxes, higher rents.

Two cottages in Warter bear the date 1858 and they would have been erected on the order of the fourth Lord Muncaster (Sir John Penington having become the first Lord Muncaster in 1783). They were built of red brick, whereas it would seem from Dr Hunter's report that the previous cottages were of a mud, timber and thatch construction, sometimes known as 'mud and stud'. However, the majority of the building work appears to have taken place in the late 1860s, shortly after the results of Dr Hunter's inquiry were published. Perhaps the poor condition of the estate being publicly reported in this way provided the impetus necessary for the new fifth Lord Muncaster to complete the work his brother had started 10 years before.

Subsequent owners of the estate made further additions so that by the end of the 19th century the estate workers of Warter had spacious, well constructed homes, most with several bedrooms, a living room, kitchen and garden. Yet the number of villagers had begun to fall. Warter Priory — the 'big house' — had been built in 1840 1.5km (1 mile) outside the village. The associated parkland and woodland, as well as the gardens of the house itself and the regular shooting parties held there, provided the main source of employment in the village but by the outbreak of the Great War the heyday of the large country house had already passed.

These days, Warter has fewer than half the residents it did at the end of the 19th century, and of this small number only a handful still work on the land although the village is still considered a farming settlement. There is only one general shop where once there were three, and there are no more shoemakers, tailors, saddlers, blacksmiths, wheelwrights or carpenters. Ironically, it seems that in the time it took for the living conditions of workers in the village to improve, the reason for them to be there had all but vanished.

*RIGHT: Warter's war memorial stands at the centre of the small triangular village green. Behind it the slender spire of the priory church of St James, rebuilt in the 19th century rises above a screen of trees.*

# THE BURTONS

## EAST YORKSHIRE

There are many pretty villages on the outskirts of Beverley, but none quite as magical as the Burtons. When the air is still and the water like glass, the village pond reflects white walls, red tiles, white clouds and blue sky with perfect clarity. It was beside this crescent mirror under a wych elm that John Wesley preached in a corner of the green known forever after as Preacher's Corner, and for many years following, villagers would hold an open-air service there in remembrance of the occasion.

In AD 708, long before the founder of Methodism complained that the Methodist church at Bishop Burton was too small, St John of Beverley consecrated the village's first church, which was probably even smaller. The present grey stone church of St Crispin, was built on the same site in the 13th century and rebuilt 6 centuries later. Previously known as Burton-by-Beverley, the village acquired the prefix 'Bishop' when the archbishops of York held the manor, built a 'palace' and had a deer park here.

Curving around the village pond, the busy and often extremely noisy A1079 York to Beverley road has brought people to the door of Bishop Burton's coaching inn for centuries. It was once called the Horse and Jockey because, since the late 18th century, the big house and park behind the pub had been operating as a stud farm, producing a string of successful racehorses. In the early 19th century, Mr Richard Watt inherited the estate from his grand-uncle (the first of three Richard Watts to be squire there), who had been a Liverpool stable boy and coach driver before making his fortune in the West Indies. In 1813, one of the Watt-bred horses won the St Leger as a 50/1 outsider and the pub acquired a new name in celebration of the event: the Altisidora. Richard Watt III was eventually to get his hands on a total of four St Legers and one Oaks but you will not find racehorses in Bishop Burton today as the stud farm is now an agricultural college.

Nor will you find Wesley's wych elm on the village green. Long before the countrywide outbreak of Dutch elm disease, this particular specimen had been struck by lightning. In 1836, Squire Watt paid for a bust of the preacher to be carved from wood cut from the felled tree. It stood for years in the Methodist chapel but, eventually, with the congregation short of funds and their place of worship in urgent need of repair, it was sold to the Anglican rector and Wesley now sits in the parish church.

In 1823, among a population dominated by farmers, there were two tailors, two boot- and shoe-makers, two shopkeepers, a blacksmith and a joiner-wheelwright working in the village. By 1892, despite an agricultural depression, there was little change apart from the presence of two 'steam thrashing machine' proprietors and the fact that, appropriately enough for a village with such a large pond, there was a 'Swann' in the schoolroom and two 'Ducks' working as joiner-wheelwrights.

Somewhat less well known, being off the main road and probably grateful for it, is Bishop Burton's little sister, Cherry. It is situated about 5km (3 miles) away and is now a certified 'Fair Trade Village', becoming only the second village in England to achieve this status. Actively promoting fairly traded and locally produced goods, the people of Cherry Burton have successfully raised awareness of the need to support small-scale village economies both at home and around the world.

*RIGHT: In the 18th century, John Wesley preached a sermon on the village green beside the pond at Bishop Burton. The busy York to Beverley road skirts the pond so any preacher visiting today might have difficulty making himself heard.*

# KIRKLEATHAM

## CLEVELAND

*A* tiny village on the outskirts of Redcar, Kirkleatham is unusual in having many large and historically important buildings but very few cottages. It was called Westlidum in 1086, yet was known as Kirkelidin a century later when the Old English prefix 'west' was replaced by the Old Scandinavian word for church an odd change so long after the time of the Vikings, who were undoubtedly once here at this 'place at the slopes'.

Kirkleatham passed through a number of hands after the Norman Conquest, including those of George, Lord Lumley, executed for his part in a conspiracy against Henry VIII in 1537, and those of Sir William Bellasis, who sold it in 1623 to a wealthy London merchant by the name of John Turner. The new owner immediately set about improving the estate by ordering the construction of Kirkleatham Hall in 1625, thus starting a family tradition of building that was to turn this little agricultural estate into a wonder of philanthropic architecture.

Turner's third son, William, was born in Kirkleatham but retraced his father's footsteps by becoming a successful London wool merchant in his own right. Knighted in 1662, he went on to hold the office of sheriff, and, in 1669, became Lord Mayor of London. In 1676, back in Kirkleatham, work was completed on Sir William Turner's Hospital, possibly the best known of all the village's grand buildings. It was not a hospital as we would know it today, but almshouses endowed with an estate that would provide for the maintenance of 40 poor people there plus a charity school.

More impressive building work followed. Further to a bequest by Sir William a free grammar school for the benefit of the children of Coatham and Kirkleatham was completed in 1709 by his nephew, Cholmley Turner, who in 1740, commissioned the Turner Mausoleum, in memory of his son Marwood. Later yet another member of the Turner dynasty, Sir Charles, developed the agricultural side of the Kirkleatham estate until it was one of the foremost in the region by the time of his death in 1810.

Unfortunately, when the direct line of descent died out, the estate fell into decline and started to be split up. The hospital endowments were placed in the hands of the charity commissioners, who, due to the agricultural depression in the latter part of the 19th century, could accommodate fewer people and the school was forced to accept non-resident children. Later, the Old Hall (the former grammar school) was used to billet soldiers during the First World War but gradually the buildings began to fall out of use.

At the instigation of the charity commissioners, who wanted some parts of the estate to be sold off, the hall was demolished in the 1950s and the hardwood trees in the parkland sold, while neglect and vandalism led to the decay of other buildings. It was not until 1970 that Teesside Borough Council realized what an asset Kirkleatham's unique collection of historic buildings could be

and a conservation area was drawn up. The council acquired the Old Hall and converted it into a popular museum, the almshouses were refurbished and the stable block was re-roofed.

Slowly, Kirkleatham is being brought back to life as a rural amenity for the people of Redcar and beyond. There are still only a few small estate workers' cottages in the area around the church (although new housing is planned), and while there is now a Kirkleatham Business Park on the outskirts of the village, there is no school or pub. The regeneration of Kirkleatham – changes in local administration permitting – will be very much based on the theme of heritage, with special emphasis on the many important listed buildings there, as well as on the existing visitor attractions, such as the museum and Owl Centre. Investment from private companies will also be required to ensure the long-term future of this very unusual but very special place.

*ABOVE: Built in 1847 beside the railway line at Redcar, the 'Railway Cottages' were later dismantled and re-erected in Kirkleatham.*

*OPPOSITE: Sir William Turner's Hospital. Founded in 1676, it has been converted into independent retirement homes for up to 30 people.*

# BRANCEPETH

## DURHAM

*he village of Brancepeth is remarkable for its picturesque appearance and pleasant situation. It is beautifully arranged, and kept in park-like order'.* History, Topography and Directory of the County Palatine of Durham, Francis Whellan, London, 1894

  Little has changed in Brancepeth since the above assessment was made. Perhaps the road that slices the village in two is busier today than it once was, and there has been some modern development, but by maintaining the 'park-like' theme this has been successfully assimilated. Stretching along a single road that crosses the A690, Brancepeth is a delight of warm golden stone, fine architectural details, cobblestones and colourful flowers.

  With a probable Roman road passing through the parish, its origins may have been as a bridgehead settlement that developed where travellers would have had to cross a river

*RIGHT: The sale of the estate in the 1960s led to a spate of new building in the vicinity of the station. Today most of Brancepeth's residents commute, some being prepared to travel considerable distances, such is the charm of the place.*

running through a deep ravine. Local legend would have us believe that the village was named after a great wild boar, or brawn, which, it is said, once roamed the nearby woods frequenting the 'Brawn's Path' although the accepted definition is 'path of a man named Brandr'.

For a village that consists of little more than a church and some cottages, Brancepath boasts an incredible wealth of history, but it also has a castle and that makes all the difference. Nor were the castle's owners content to sit back and enjoy the magnificent view: when they made their various marks on history, feudal custom dictated that a number of Brancepeth villagers went with them.

The castle was begun in the 12th century by the Bulmers, a powerful Saxon family that had survived the Norman Conquest and the subsequent 'harrying' of the north virtually unscathed. When

Emma Bulmer married Geoffrey de Neville of Horncastle, a great Saxon family was joined with a noble Norman one.

There was a Neville at the signing of Magna Carta in 1215. Another fought in France at the side of Edward III and defeated the Scottish king, David, at the Battle of Neville's Cross in 1341, while in 1385 John Neville was made Admiral of the Fleet, later marching into Scotland alongside Richard II at the head of a fighting force of 200 men, many of whom had been stationed at Brancepeth. The rise of the Nevilles seemed unstoppable. In 1397, Ralph Neville was given the title Earl of Westmorland by Richard II. Even so, Ralph went on to play a significant role in the political manoeuvring through which the crown was usurped by his brother-in-law, the Duke of Lancaster (Henry IV). Appointed Marshal of England, Ralph would later take 5 knights, 30 horses and 80 archers from Brancepeth to Agincourt with Henry V.

The 14th century had been good to the Nevilles. However, the Reformation forced many noble families to choose between loyalty to the crown or their faith. Determined see a return to Catholicism, Charles Neville, together with the Earl of Northumberland, planned the 'Rising of the North', massing a great army at Brancepeth in 1569. The rebellion failed, Neville fled, and Brancepeth was confiscated by the Crown. Thereafter, besides providing 1,400 oak trees for the construction of the first triple-decker warship in the English fleet, the village played no further part in the nation's history.

At the end of the 18th century, William Russell, a Sunderland banker and coalmine owner, purchased the estate and made the castle his home. Consequently, no mining took place in the immediate vicinity, and Brancepeth was once described as 'a rural gem in an industrial setting'. Today, the castle and its estate remain the main employers in the village, along with the golf course, which was established in the castle grounds in 1924. Recently the community has been united in the restoration of its 12th-century church, virtually destroyed by fire in 1999.

# GAINFORD

## DURHAM

So successfully has Gainford managed to hide its 3-acre green that many people passing quickly through the village on the busy main road from Darlington to Barnard Castle are probably unaware that they are missing one of the loveliest village greens in County Durham. Sloping from High Green in the north to Low Green in the south, Gainford's roughly rectangular stretch of grass – so characteristic of greens in the area, with its scattering of fine trees and ancient market cross – is enclosed on all four sides by houses. Such an arrangement in an area once troubled by Scottish incursions has given rise to the belief that the village must have been laid out in this way intentionally as a defensive measure: since the only access points are at the four corners, barricaded livestock could be kept safely in the central grassy enclosure until danger passed. Yet this remains a theory, and one to which there is some opposition.

The smart street of 18th-century buildings at High Green quite literally look down on the more typical dark gritstone dwellings that line the other three sides. However, probably the most attractive group of buildings is to be found away from the green altogether. The uneven roofline of a curved terrace of colour-washed houses in an assortment of

heights and hues is situated along a lane called High Row, which is carved into the hillside. Below, in their shadow, sits a delightful group of cottages on the wonderfully named Piggy Lane, which brings to mind a snippet of local folklore. This tells of a vicar of Gainford who is supposed to have married a Pigg, christened a Lamb and buried a Hogg on three consecutive Saturdays.

To the west is Gainford Hall, built in 1600. It is a marvellous Grade I-listed building, with an interesting group of 11 chimneys in the centre of its roof. The oldest structure in the village is St Mary's Church at the south-western corner of the green. The church that we see today is late Norman, but it was built on the site of an extensive Anglo-Saxon monastery founded by Egred, Bishop of Lindesfarne, in the 9th century AD. The monastic complex lay near an ancient fording place of the River Tees and may have stretched far further than the boundaries of the present churchyard as human bones were discovered beneath the green in the 18th century, a possible indication that it had once been part of the cemetery. Fragments of stone carvings unearthed in the village dating from that time show both Danish and Anglo-Saxon influence, so it is probable that the two cultures mixed in this area, perhaps as a result of the important river crossing.

Later, the village became an important market centre, its prosperity clearly indicated by several good 18th-century properties. By the 19th century, the ford had become a ferry and Gainford even had its own spa. For a time the village was virtually self-sufficient: a small, self-contained community supporting numerous local craftsmen. However, the wonderful scenery all around soon made it a popular choice for Darlington retirees. Recent modern expansion has largely taken place north of the A67 in an area where, before the 20th century, there were only a handful of buildings and an old railway line (since dismantled), so the old core of the village has been left almost intact. Although the village now boasts a modern school, doctor's surgery, hairdresser's, takeaway, three pubs and several other thriving businesses, it is nice to see that the old ways are still appreciated, for the village has a traditional shoemaker who crafts fine footwear by hand. His craftsmanship is so sought-after that he has a two-month waiting list.

ABOVE: *The Cross Keys Inn stands at the end of the uneven terrace of houses known as High Row; the other pub in the village is the Lord Nelson.*

# WHITBURN

## TYNE & WEAR

**W**hitburn's survival as an extremely pretty coastal village squeezed between the two massive conurbations of Sunderland and South Shields seems nothing less than miraculous. There are now strict preservation orders in force to safeguard its future, but just how the village survived in the days before official intervention of this kind was available, or even considered desirable can be explained only by its geographical position.

Situated on the coast and separated from Sunderland by the sea, with no through road and very few connecting ones, Whitburn has remained mercifully isolated and therefore relatively unspoilt. There has been modern development here, of course – there is a council estate on the edge of the village, for example – but the historic core

LEFT: *Irrepressibly ornate, if perhaps a little overdone, Whitburn House was constructed in the mid-19th century. Opposite stood 17th-century Whitburn Hall, which by the late 1980s had become dangerously dilapidated and was subsequently demolished.*

of small late 17th- and early 18th-century cottages and later Georgian houses remains virtually untouched.

First recorded in 1190, Whitburn means 'tumulus or barn of a man named Hwita'. Originally a Saxon settlement, it was rebuilt in Norman times around a long village green to become a typical medieval village following a 'three-field system' of cultivation. Fore Street is the main street, connected to the Back Lane by a series of lanes running between the two, while East Street comprises mainly farms and farm buildings to this day. To the west, the old village meets the modern estate just past Glebe Farm.

A farming and fishing community throughout its long history, Whitburn boasts an impressive list of typical village features. There is a village well, pond, green, inn, windmill and pinfold (a pound for stray animals). Once there were two dairy herds here; driven through the village twice a day, they would often stop for a drink at the pond before moving on.

Whitburn Hall, a large 17th-century property that was once the home of Sir Hedworth Williamson, became so dilapidated that it was eventually pulled down. But there is still the Victorian Whitburn House (gamely pretending to be Elizabethan) to enjoy and two of the three old pubs survive – the Grey Horse and the Jolly Sailor – both of which are going strong; the Highlander was removed during road-widening in the 1930s. With its faux Victorian lamp posts and imitation half-timbering – a fad briefly shared by the Jolly Sailor pub at one time – Whitburn is in danger of disguising its true antiquity.

Lewis Carroll is said to have received inspiration for characters in his 'Alice' books from people he encountered during his many stays in the village, and in a place where things are not always quite what they seem it is hardly surprising. Today, with a parade of attractive shops, a post office, bank and doctor's surgery, the little community is largely self-contained. It also has a busy social calendar. There is a cricket team and an annual festival plus many clubs and societies, including a well run local history group.

Whitburn Colliery was a mining settlement almost 2.5km (1.5 miles) to the north of the village. In 1874, the Harton Coal Company, which had been operating pits in the South Shields area since the 1840s, set up the Whitburn Coal Company to exploit the coastal coal reserves. Also known as Marsden Colliery, the first pit was sunk in the late 1870s in an area near the Souter Lighthouse. A new village was built for the miners near the old hamlet at Marsden, but its exposed clifftop location meant that many of the miners preferred to live either in South Shields or in Whitburn itself. The Whitburn Coal Company also purchased the existing lighthouse lime quarries, and to improve communications with South Shields a railway line was laid down to link the company's various operations. After nearly a century of successful production, Whitburn Colliery closed in 1968 and the purpose-built village was demolished; the residents being relocated nearer to the village of Whitburn.

Meanwhile the fishing activity at Whitburn was carried out in an attached hamlet called Whitburn Bents, which has altered little during more than 200 years. Fishermen now have the red- and white-striped Souter Lighthouse as a landmark, but for centuries before that they relied on the late Norman tower of St Mary Magdalene Church, Whitburn.

# DOWNHAM

## LANCASHIRE

nyone who has seen the classic 1960s film *Whistle Down The Wind* already knows Downham. It has that supremely relaxed quality that people identify with a traditional English village. You can easily imagine that those fortunate enough to live here do so without the aid of clocks and watches, simply rising and retiring with the sun and shaking their heads at the rest of us poor souls for whom time matters.

Downham is a wonderfully uncluttered place, the warm brown-stone cottages all the more charming for their simplicity. A wide road sweeps through the centre of the village, past the upper green on the brow of the hill and down alongside the long lower green with its small stream and small bridges. It then takes you back out into the rolling farmland that shelters in the lee of a huge whale-back hill.

It would be tempting to think that Downham has always been a place of sublime rural tranquility and yet 400 years ago it could be quite a dangerous place. Lancashire has the reputation of having been a very superstitious county (in fact, there are those that say it still is!) and the strange-shaped hill, so green and benign, has a troubled past. For it is Pendle: the hill of the witches. It was said that Downham Old Hall con-

tained a secret chamber, the purported hiding place of Alice Nutter, who was later tried and hanged at Lancaster with nine other 'Pendle Witches'. Alice was meant to have worked her dark magic on the noble family of Assheton who resided there. Today, the Old Hall is an impressive but very aged farmhouse; in 1612, it was the manor house.

Perhaps this 'place at the hills' is indeed bewitched, for apart from the occasional car, there is an absence of modern intrusions. There are no television aerials or overhead cables (a boon for the television companies that visit). There are no pavements or painted lines, the quiet lanes being shared between pedestrian and vehicle in good-natured fashion. In Downham, ducks and children paddle together under the bridges, then wander across the quiet road in rare safety. It is a scene from the days when cars and metalled byways were unknown in these parts and the horse-drawn cart held sway. Much of the credit belongs to the inhabitants of this enchanting village, who clearly tend it well, but it was the Assheton family that built much that we can see. For more than four centuries they have involved themselves in the life of the village and actively nurtured their creation.

Amidst a pastoral landscape of great beauty, we find Elizabethan weavers' cottages and a school built in 1839, although Downham has had a school since the 16th century. There is a neat post office and a working forge that produces traditional anvil-formed ironware as well as contemporary sculptural designs. At the heart of the village, still exerting their influence over the lives of the villagers, is the classic triumvirate of church, inn and manor house, where an Assheton resides to this day.

# WYCOLLER

## LANCASHIRE

*L*overs of all things supernatural flock to Wycoller to thrill at stories of 'The Blue Lady' of Pierson House or the mysterious figure dressed in black who glides from the ruins of Wycoller Hall to the packhorse bridge; not to mention the poltergeist at Wycoller House, or the huntsman dressed in Stuart costume, thought to be a former squire held responsible for the death (some say murder) of his wife.

Yet the real interest of this lovely yet enigmatic village lies in its more tangible features, all of which clearly indicate a long human presence here. Once a royal hunting ground complete with deer, wolves and wild boar, Wycoller was primarily an agricultural settlement until the 18th century with sheep farming and weaving as its mainstays. Vaccary walling from the 14th century survives to this day: perhaps the very same 'sheep walls' that were recorded in an inquisition of 1311, and weavers' 'wuzzing' holes, where the water was spun from a bobbinful of wet wool pressed against a hard surface, can be seen worn into the wall of Pierson House.

Wycoller Hall, built for the Hartley family at the close of the 16th century, fell into disrepair following the death in 1818 of its debt-ridden owner, Henry Owen Cunliffe

and is now no more than a romantic ruin. Most of the cottages in Wycoller are also more than three centuries old and display many original features. In 1820, the village had a population of 350, but growing industrialization eventually forced the weavers to move to the towns, hoping to find employment in the mills. Empty properties soon fell derelict; the stone from their walls (and from the derelict Hall) being re-used elsewhere in the village. As many as 35 dwellings 'disappeared' in this way, yet those that survived have been lovingly restored and give an idea of just how magical the place must have been in its heyday.

Wycoller Beck, which runs through the centre of the village, is crossed by no fewer than seven bridges, of which three are particularly interesting. Now scheduled as an Ancient Monument the Iron Age Clam Bridge is a single enormous slab of gritstone, while the late 18th-century Clapper Bridge (sometimes known as Druid's Bridge) is no more than three gritstone slabs resting on two supports. It is said that grooves worn into its surface by the clogs of weavers were chiselled flat by a farmer whose daughter was fatally injured there in 1912. Meanwhile, Sally's Bridge, named after the mother of the last squire, is a twin-arched packhorse bridge that has stood, in one form or another, for the past 900 years.

In the 1890s the village narrowly escaped being submerged by a reservoir. Public pressure forced a search for an alternative new water supply and thankfully a large underground spring was discovered just in time. Wycoller is now little more than a hamlet catering to the needs of its many visitors, while the surrounding area has been designated as a country park. A magnificent 17th-century aisled barn has found new purpose as a hi-tech interactive visitors' centre while the craft centre in the village has a traditional tea room with an open Victorian range. There are no other shops, no pub, no school and no church, and there probably never will be, but Wycoller is a wonderful example of a village that has narrowly avoided extinction.

*OPPOSITE: Identified as the inspiration for Ferndean Manor in Charlotte Bronte's novel* Jane Eyre *Wycoller Hall was still largely intact as recently as the early 1900s.*

*BELOW: Pierson House is reputedly visited by a spectral Grey Lady who passes through the wall into the adjoining Wycoller Farm.*

# CALDBECK

## CUMBRIA

*A*typical stone-built Cumbrian village, Caldbeck lies in a remote area dominated by the mountain peaks of Skiddaw and High Pike, and owes its existence to two important factors: there are rich deposits of lead, copper and byrites (barium sulphate) in the area; and it is here that Cald Beck (a stream) and the River Caldew unite. Mining of the fells behind the village may have started as early as the 13th century, but the industry reached its high point 300–400 years later. Such was the mineral wealth of the region that a popular saying was coined: 'Caldbeck and the Caldbeck Fells are worth all England else'. By 1795, there were nearly 1,800 people living in the village, which had become a near self-sufficient community, its members following many diverse trades. It was

*RIGHT: Set beneath the Northern Fells of the Lake District, a group of quaint cottages sit prettily behind colourful gardens that spill down into the cold beck, from which this traditional fell village gets its name.*

around this time that a large number of the cottages in the centre of the village were built.

With such an abundance of water power, it is hardly surprising to find that Caldbeck possessed many mills for processing corn, wool, bobbins and paper. Priest's Mill, recently restored and converted into a mining museum, was built by the rector in 1702 as a corn mill for the church. Many of the other mills in the village are now private homes, while one is being used as the workshop of a maker of traditional clogs.

Built to supply the Lancashire weavers Caldbeck's 19th-century bobbin mill was 800m (0.5 mile) from the centre of the village at the Howk, a beautiful limestone gorge with a tree-shaded waterfall. The mill's massive wheel, measuring 90cm (3 feet) wide and 13m (42 feet) in diameter, was the largest in the country and the second largest in the world at the time. Work stopped there in 1924 and the big wheel has gone, but the ruins of the buildings remain.

Yet this community is far older than it may at first appear. Across the 15th-century packhorse bridge and behind the church of St Kentigern, lies St Mungo's well, which was used in the 6th century AD for early Christian baptisms. Kentigern and Mungo were one and the same person, and he is said to have preached in Caldbeck when travelling from Scotland to Wales in AD 533. His church, however, stands on a Norman foundation. In the graveyard lie the subjects of two popular ballads.

'D'ye ken John Peel with his coat so grey' became one of the best-loved songs of its day. It was penned by John Graves who was well acquainted with Peel, for the two men would often hunt foxes together out on the fells, frequently on foot. Peel's prowess as a huntsman was legendary in the area – as was his temper.

The other celebrated resident was Mary Robinson, also known as the Maid of Buttermere, a young woman so beautiful people would travel from far and wide just to catch a glimpse of her face; Wordsworth wrote a poem about her. Yet unwittingly she married a notorious forger and fraudster who, less than a year after the wedding, was hanged for his crimes. Her second marriage, to a steady Caldbeck farmer, was more successful, while her life story became the subject of ballads and other works of popular entertainment.

Today, Caldbeck's historic core is protected by a preservation order. Ponies and sheep wander freely about the village or pause to drink from a duck pond that was once an old clay pit. Known as 'clay-dubs', it supported the local brick and tile works. The old brewery, which at one time supplied 16 alehouses, still stands, although it has been converted for residential use and there is now only one pub, a fine 17th-century coaching inn called the Oddfellows Arms. It seems that the whole place, exhausted by centuries of frantic industrial activity, has slipped gracefully into retirement.

# GRASMERE

## CUMBRIA

Grasmere is in the unusual position of being overshadowed by both the surrounding scenery and one of its former inhabitants. Architecturally, this rather odd place has little to recommend it. There are some pleasant enough roughstone cottages fashioned from the traditional building material of the area – an attractive blue-green Lakeland slate – and a church. The latter, dedicated to St Oswald, the 7th-century Christian king of Northumbria, was once described as 'large and massy for duration built', which pretty well sums it up. But it is to pay homage to the man who penned those words that people flock to Grasmere by the coachload today.

William Wordsworth and his sister Dorothy lived in a small outlying part of the village in the former Dove and Olive Branch inn, at that time known simply as Town End (it did not become the famous Dove Cottage until much later). Visitors to the

OPPOSITE: *Grasmere's situation in one of the most dramatically picturesque parts of the Lake District could hardly be bettered.*

BELOW: *Much of the village dates from the 19th century although the old village school and some cottages are 17th-century.*

house included friends such as Coleridge and Sir Walter Scott, and it was here that Wordsworth wrote some of his best-loved poetry.

Grasmere without the Wordsworth connection would undoubtedly be a very different place from the one we see today. The spectacular scenery and the captivating lake with its central island would always be a draw, of course; Wordsworth's muse was the landscape around Grasmere and he was not the first to feel its magic. The Norsemen were here first and cleared the land by a glassy mere that would one day become known as Grass Lake, or Grasmere while 1.5km (1 mile) or so to the south, a settlement took shape in the valley of the River Rothay, beneath the copper-green slopes of Helm Crag and Nab Scar.

In August, crowds gather to see children from the village perform the ancient rush-bearing ceremony, which recalls the days when the floor of the church was beaten earth strewn liberally with rushes. August is also the month for the Grasmere Sports, when fell-running and Cumberland wrestling, among other events, pull in vast numbers of spectators. But it is for Wordsworth that most make the journey to Grasmere. Whether he would be pleased to see what the village has become in his name is moot. He was a man who loved simplicity above all things, and, although he would probably be gratified to learn that so many had gained employment as a result of his efforts, it is doubtful that he would have enjoyed all the fuss. This was a man who, despite being Poet Laureate and thus entitled to an abbey tomb, chose instead to be buried in a plain churchyard grave in a little Lakeland village.

# BLANCHLAND

## NORTHUMBERLAND

Blanchland appears as if from nowhere, whichever road you choose to take you there. But the descent from the moors to the south and across the old stone bridge over the River Derwent must surely offer the most picturesque first glimpse of one of Northumberland's loveliest villages.

In 1165, Walter de Bolbec, who held the manor here, granted some land on the river's north bank to an order of Premonstratensian monks, or 'White Canons'. The name Blanchland actually means 'white wooded glade', but most people believe it refers to the white robes of the monks who built an abbey on the site. 'Blanchelande' was theirs until its dissolution in 1539, although intermittent border raids by the Scots had by that time left scars on the place.

So it was slightly the worse for wear that Blanchland passed into the hands of the Radcliffe family, from whom it was purchased in 1623 by the Forsters of Bamburgh, who possibly used it as a hunting lodge. Nearly 80 years later, Lord Crewe, Bishop of Durham, married Dorothy Forster and soon afterwards purchased what remained of Blanchland Abbey from her family, which, due to its owner's dire financial position, had suffered years of neglect. When the bishop died in 1721, his estates, including Blanchland, were left in the hands of trustees, the income from them to be distributed

*RIGHT: Visitors to the Lord Crewe Arms can ask to be shown the priest's hole in which Thomas Forster, one of the leaders of the Jacobite rebellion in 1715, and nephew of Lady Crewe, is said to have hidden from government forces.*

BELOW LEFT: *The combined village Post Office and shop occupies part of Blanchland's magnificent crenellated medieval gate house.*

BELOW: *Set in a secluded glen deep in the Derwent Valley, Blanchland is a beautiful example of early planned industrial housing.*

between various worthy institutions.

John Wesley described Blanchland Abbey as 'little more than a heap of ruins' when he preached there in 1747, but the trustees began intense restoration work only a few years later. While retaining much of the original site plan, they ranged rows of new houses around the L-shaped courtyard that had once fronted the monks' accommodation. Solidly built in attractive grey-brown sandstone, these were to be the homes of lead miners working on the estate, and as such they represent an early – and particularly attractive – example of a planned industrial village. Similar properties were constructed on the other side of the cobbled gateway, with the monks' former refectory and guest house becoming the Lord Crewe Arms (traces of the cloisters can be found in its garden) while the 13th-century chancel of the abbey church was rebuilt to serve as the parish church of St Mary.

Blanchland is no longer a village of miners, the main local employer being the Lord Crewe Arms Hotel, while many of the residents are retired and the remainder work outside the village. The monks' water mill at the bridge has gone, a post office has been fitted neatly into the old abbey gatehouse, the Lord Crewe Arms has acquired a fair selection of ghosts, including the mysteriously named 'Grey Lady of Derwent Water', and there is now a White Monk Tea Rooms and a Blanchland Stores. But the trustees still control the estate, and somehow the tranquility of a medieval abbey has been retained. Quite unlike any other village in the area, Blanchland's unique charm and magnificent location hidden in the wild heather moors lend it a romance that is hard to equal.

# ELSDON

## NORTHUMBERLAND

ronze Age farmers created the fields here, building great cairns from the stones they cleared. They made their round houses in this sheltered hollow with its little burn and buried their dead in yet more cairns. The traces remain for us to discover today. However, later evidence of defended Iron Age settlements provides the first clue that there might have been more happening here than peaceful communities simply farming the beautiful fells.

After the Conquest, William realised that a stable, well defended border was the key to lucrative trade with the north and would create a check to any action by exiled Anglo-Saxon nobles who had crossed into Scotland. At that time the main road into Scotland from England was, as it had been for centuries, an old Roman road called Dene Street, which ran through an area of Northumberland known as Redesdale. And so in 1080, a motte-and-bailey castle was built at Elsdon as part of William's

northern defences, but its remote location made it ineffective and a century later it was superseded by a castle at Harbottle 16km (10 miles) distant. Harbottle became the stronghold of the de Umphraville family, Lords of Redesdale, and Elsdon became their administrative centre. By the Middle Ages, the small village that had grown up in the shadow of its Norman castle had become the capital of the entire region – a position it retained until the packhorse trading routes and cattle droves marked by ancient wayside crosses fell out of use in the 19th century.

From the 13th century, annual fairs and weekly markets were held on the seven-acre village green around Elsdon's 12th-century church. Nevertheless, border raids continued unabated and throughout the medieval period, battles continued to rage between the English and the Scots, as did feuds between rival clans within the region itself. Villagers must have spent a good deal of their lives in fear and this is reflected in the architecture of the region. Houses in the shape of defensive structures, known as Pele Towers, were built by whoever could afford them and Elsdon has a particularly fine example. But Elsdon was very much a frontier town and its inhabitants not merely the innocent victims of the lawless, for in 1498 the Bishop of Durham complained that the village was full of 'reivers and cattle lifters'.

Elsdon is a quiet, attractive place today but every now and then there is a reminder of the region's bloody past. In the 19th century, a mass grave was discovered in the churchyard, with 100 skeletons ranged neatly in two rows, thought to be the remains of men who fell at the Battle of Otterburn in 1388.

# THE QUINTESSENTIAL ENGLISH VILLAGE

## BIDDESTONE
WILTSHIRE

*BELOW: Behind the war memorial stands an attractive row of 18th-century houses. Slate and tile roofs predominate in Biddestone, only a handful of thatched cottages remain.*

**D**id I find the quintessential English village? Well, yes and no.

'Yes' because this search was about more than ticking off items on a list. It was an attempt to discover whether the notion of the 'typical' English village had become a piece of folklore, or if, in fact, it had ever been anything more than that. Reassuringly, I found that there is still much of real beauty and charm in England's villages, yet our peculiar relationship with these places remains as complex as ever. Any dissatisfaction we might feel with the reality of today's English villages is as much a product of our unrealistic, media-fed expectations as of any shortcomings in the places themselves. Bar a smattering of notable exceptions, villages were not designed to be aesthetically appealing: they have evolved over the centuries, constantly adapting to ever-changing circumstances in a struggle to survive. If anything, then, the defining quality of the best of our villages is strength of character rather than visual attractiveness or great age.

And 'No' because we cannot concentrate on form alone: much of what constitutes an English village belongs to the world of emotion. No combination of pond and green or pub and church, and no amount of brick, flint, tile, thatch, half-timbering and plaster will ever feel exactly 'right'. No matter how close we as individuals might come to finding our own quintessential English village, there will always be others who will disagree with our selection and have every right to argue the superiority of their choice. English villages are so essentially regional in character, appearance, layout and setting that to find one that is a satisfactory summation would be to deny all that is so worthwhile in local individuality. Nearly all of the very different villages to be found within the pages of this book have been described as a 'typical English village' at some point!

My own personal choice would be Biddestone in Wiltshire. It has a pleasant open central area with a quiet road running through the middle of the large village green. To one side a perfectly proportioned pond complete with ducks of several varieties and a pair of geese ripples next to a traditional-looking inn with a traditional-sounding name: the White Horse. An assortment of mellow stone

cottages, some of them thatched and many of them constructed in the 1700s, interspersed with a handful of grander dwellings, line the edges of the green and spill down the roadways, lanes and tracks that lead off to the neighbouring villages and the surrounding fields.

There are in fact two village pubs, for the Biddestone Arms can be found along the road that leads to the fine 17th-century manor house with its beautiful formal gardens. There were also two churches here once, both of them with Saxon origins, although one is now a romantic ruin, while only that of St Nicholas survives. By the church gate, the village pump stands beneath a quaint tiled roof while close by, farmyards open right into the heart of the village.

On a quiet morning with few cars around to break the spell it takes almost no imagination to slip back through the years and picture the bustle of village life as it must once have been. Livestock grazing the green or drinking from the pond would have been a common sight for the village lay on the drove road from Bristol. And let us not forget the villagers themselves: people at work or fetching water from the pump; some visiting the shop and others the pub; people outside their cottages, cleaning, repairing or simply chatting; and children racing to school or minding the animals.

Yet even here the dream is in danger of fading. Within the last six years, the village shop closed down and the school quickly followed. But these losses are sufficiently recent that their impact is not immediately obvious to the visitor, and there is an extremely strong community in Biddestone whose hard work and imaginative efforts have been rewarded with the opening of a new village hall and sports pavilion, while the annual fair at the end of June remains one not to be missed. There may well be prettier villages, but this was never a search for the quaint-essential English village, and for me, despite the lack of school and shop, Biddestone is about as close to my personal idea of the quintessential English village as I am likely to get.

In the fabled English village it is per-

petual high summer. The sun beats down on white-clad cricketers, permanently occupying the green under the benevolent gaze of an ancient church. There are no cars, although a vintage one might just be permissible. Bees hum eternally around the honeysuckle, hollyhocks nod drowsily and roses drape themselves luxuriantly over rustic porches while ducks cool their feet in the pond and starlings tug at a stray piece of thatch. Only at Christmas time does this imaginary village change its appearance, when it instantly acquires a thick blanket of snow and suddenly becomes infested with cheerful robins. What real village could possibly live up to expectations such as these?

In reality, the English village is busy reinventing itself for the 21st century. In places it has taken an influx of 'townies' to boost beleaguered spirits, but villages can think of this phenomenon as the return of the sons and daughters (albeit a few generations down the line) that they

*ABOVE: In winter, when the pond is solidly frozen, villagers have been known to use it as a skating rink. A large flat stone by its side may be the base of an old ducking stool.*

lost in the great agricultural depression of the late 19th century, when the fields almost emptied into the towns. Many incomers feel as passionately about the preservation of the school, the fabric of the church and the state of the grass on the green, and worry just as much about incongruous new-builds and unsightly extensions as the few villagers who can trace an unbroken occupancy back to feudal times. Just as important, new residents frequently bring with them skills honed in the high-pressure world of commerce not to mention being usefully fluent in the language of bureaucracy.

Eminently pragmatic, villagers have always understood, perhaps more clearly than the rest of us, the necessity of change although these days there is also a growing awareness of our heritage as a non-renewable resource. It is difficult to strike the right balance, but the Countryside Agency, National Trust and English Heritage are each playing their part in protecting the oldest and most fragile elements of our rural landscapes. Councils have designated Conservation Areas, and the new Village Design Statements and Parish Plans must be viewed as a step in the right direction. Moreover, village organisations have dis-

covered that the Internet can be used not only as a local celebration of community and heritage or as a marketing opportunity to draw in visitors, but also as a link with other villages across the country that have faced (or are facing) similar issues. In the fight to retain vital services, the Internet has allowed for a pooling of campaign strategies. An informal inter-village support network is growing steadily and an increasing number of villages now have their own websites and discussion forums.

Ultimately, rural regeneration schemes aside, tourism appears to offer the brightest future for many communities. Today the lure of the English village is, if anything, stronger than ever, despite the depredations of recent years, and although the myth that such settlements represent idyllic environments of unchanging stability has now been exploded they do contain, nonetheless, an inherent thread of continuity that reaches back into the distant past fuelling our romantic vision of a simpler time when daily life was intimately connected with the rhythms of nature - an understandably beguiling notion when the pace, complexity and stresses of modern life can so often seem overwhelming.

*RIGHT: The White Horse pub, slate-roofed and with its old stone walls smartly whitewashed, occupies a central position on the southern edge of the green. A second pub, the Biddestone Arms, can be found close by on the Corsham Road.*

# FURTHER READING

Allingham, Hellen and Dick, Stewart, *The Cottage Homes of England* (Bracken Books, 1984; first published by Edward Arnold, 1909)

Blythe, Ronald, *Akenfield: Portrait of an English village* (Penguin Books Ltd, 1972)

Brunskill, R W, *Traditional Buildings of Britain: An Introduction to Vernacular Architecture*, 3rd edition (Cassell, 2004)

Burke, John, *English Villages* (B T Batsford Ltd, 1975)

Finberg, Joscelyne, *Exploring Villages* (Routledge & Kegan Paul, 1958)

Hammond, J L and Barbara, *The Village Labourer 1760-1832* (Longmans, Green & Co., 1911)

Jennings, Paul, *The Living Village: A picture of rural life from village scrapbooks* (Hodder & Stoughton Ltd, 1968)

Mills, A D, *Oxford Dictionary of English Place-names* (Oxford University Press, 1998)

Muir, Richard, *The Lost Villages of Britain* (Michael Joseph, 1986)

Muir, Richard, *The English Village* (Thames & Hudson, 1980)

Porter, Valerie, *Life Behind the Cottage Door* (Whittet Books Ltd, 1992)

Thompson, Flora (Dewhurst, Keith ed.) *Lark Rise to Candleford* (Nelson Thornes, 1980)

Useful Websites
National Trust, The
http://www.nationaltrust.org.uk
English Heritage
http://www.english-heritage.org.uk
Countryside Agency, The
http://www.countryside.gov.uk
English Villages
http://www.eng-villages.co.uk

# INDEX

Page numbers in *italics* refer to illustrations.